YOU CAN MASTER LIFE

YOU CAN MASTER LIFE

BY

JAMES GORDON GILKEY, M.A., D.D.

*Minister of the South Congregational Church of
Springfield, Massachusetts*

NEW YORK
THE MACMILLAN COMPANY
1935

SET UP BY BROWN BROTHERS LINOTYPERS
PRINTED IN THE UNITED STATES OF AMERICA
BY THE FERRIS PRINTING COMPANY

TO
CALMA AND LOUISE

*In memory of
a brave Christmas*

FOREWORD

ANYONE who studies people carefully soon discovers that the major difference between them is not that some have hardships, while others do not. All of us have hardships, obvious or secret. The major difference between people is that some succeed in mastering life, while others permit life to master them.

This book, like three which have preceded it,[1] discusses familiar personal problems and points out ways by which everyday individuals have succeeded, and still succeed, in solving them. The book is written in the conviction that all of us, whatever the peculiarities of our temperament or the complexities of our situation, can—to some measure at least—win this victory. The wisdom we need is offered us by men and women who have faced problems like ours, solved them, and left behind a record of their technique. The strength we need is already present

[1] *Secrets of Effective Living, Solving Life's Everyday Problems, Managing One's Self.* The Macmillan Co., 1927, 1930, 1932.

within us, in the form of a latent courage which the will-to-conquer speedily discloses. The incentive and endurance we need are, we Christians believe, provided by a Kindly God who is always seeking to help us; and who brings His aid not by changing our external situation but by quickening our inner powers.

Why life compels us to face so many problems and encounter such heavy hardships we may never fully understand. But experience shows that, even if we cannot wholly explain life, we can master it.

J. G. G.

April, 1934
Springfield, Massachusetts.

CONTENTS

YOU CAN MASTER LIFE

CHAPTER I

CONQUERING THE SENSE OF INSIGNIFICANCE

I

RECENTLY one of our American astronomers [1] made this frankly disconcerting statement. "We human beings are small in every way. We are minute in material content, microscopic against the vastness of Space, evanescent in the sweep of Time. We are little in foresight, shrivelled in spirit, inconsequential in every respect except the complexity of our chemical reactions. And consider the unimpressive circumstances of our racial origin. This Earth on which we dwell appeared only a few thousand million years ago. Originally it was merely a fragment of gas thrown off from the parent Sun. In the cold of stellar Space the gas liquefied, gradually a crust formed upon it, eventually a green mould appeared

[1] Professor Harlow Shapley.

1

in certain spots on the crust, and now the human race is here. Yet we strut about, speculate, and discuss how we can improve things! The thing that appalls me as an astronomer is not the bigness of the universe but the smallness of human beings." Multitudes of our contemporaries, learning the facts disclosed by modern science, eventually adopt this attitude. Against the vast background of Time and Space, and amid the resistless surge of Nature's colossal energies, how insignificant our race appears! How utterly trivial the individual human being!

Usually the sense of our own unimportance is deepened when we turn from a study of the universe to a study of the work we do and the place we fill in society. In all frankness most of us follow careers that are painfully unimpressive. Our daily life is made up of trivial, routine tasks; we know only a few of the people by whom we are surrounded; and only a few of them have the slightest interest in us. More disconcerting still, we eventually discover we are in the grip of vast, impersonal forces over which humanity has little or no control. Mark Twain used to say jocularly that everyone talked about the weather but that no one did anything about it. The weather is not the only thing about which we do, and can do, literally nothing. Before the relentless powers of life and death, heredity and coincidence, we are equally helpless. Caught in the grip of economic processes such as those that have swept the world since 1929 we are similarly impotent. It is this weakness of our race, this ineffectiveness of human effort, which many contemporary poets emphasize incessantly. Consider these ingenious lines, recently published by one of our most influential writers.

> Where, without bloodshed, can there be
> A more relentless enmity
> Than the long feud fought silently
>
> Between man and the growing grass?
> Man's the aggressor, for he has
> Weapons to humble and harass
>
> The impudent spears that charge upon
> His sacred privacy of lawn.
> He mows them down . . . and they are gone.
>
> His are the triumphs, till that day
> There's no more grass to cut away;
> Then—tired of labor, tired of play,

Having exhausted every whim—
He stretches out each conquering limb,
And the small grass covers him.[2]

Death and the grass finally triumphant: what a picture of human weakness and futility!

But do such poets and astronomers consider all the facts? Centuries ago Jesus watched a group of Galilean children, and then said to his friends, "Do not despise these little ones. It is not the will of your Father in heaven that one of them should perish." [3] Jesus was convinced that every human being, no matter how small or weak or insignificant, is of supreme value. Jesus believed that the ultimate destiny of each human being is a matter of profound concern to God Himself. Around those ideas the system of Christian teaching and Christian philanthropy has gradually been built. Are these central ideas in Christianity sound? Have we any real reason for believing, with Jesus, that human beings are supremely important?

[2] Louis Untermeyer, "Long Feud," from *Burning Bush.* Harcourt, Brace and Company, Inc. By permission of the publishers.
[3] Matthew 18:10, 14.

II

The next time you are troubled by the sense of insignificance, recall this fairly obvious fact. However small and weak you seem, you still possess powers which lift you above everything in the non-human and subhuman realms. What are those powers? Here is a man standing beside Niagara. In many ways the swirling stream is more impressive than he. It is bigger, stronger, older. It will be here in all its stupendous majesty long after he is dead and forgotten. Yet in other ways, and apparently more significant ways, the man has an advantage over the river. To begin with, he knows he is there by the side of the stream. The river has, as far as we can discover, not even a glimmer of self-consciousness. Furthermore the man can think about Niagara: Niagara cannot reverse the process and think about the man. Most important of all, the man can devise means by which to tame the river and harness its colossal energies. He can build a hydro-electric plant, generate electric current, and eventually banish darkness from the homes of a thousand of his fellow-creatures. Such intelligent, purposeful, creative activity is impossible for the stream. Here is the basis in reason for our Christian belief in the supreme importance of human beings. When all is said that can be said about the smallness, the weakness, and the apparent temporariness of people, people still possess powers not paralleled by anything else in creation. It is humanity's possession of these unique powers which gives humanity its unique importance and value. Recently an American professor, famous for his cynical gibes, said to his students, "Astronomically considered, man is rather unimpressive." To which a fellow-professor, far more discerning, made the obvious and devastating reply, "Astronomically considered, man is the astronomer."

Another fact we may well recall when we are burdened by the sense of insignificance is this. However small and unimportant we seem, we are profoundly significant factors in the lives of other people. What we do, what we say, even what we think are matters of grave concern to them. Consider, for example, what your work means to those who depend upon you. If you do that work faithfully and well, if you meet the expectations of those whose lives are bound up with yours, they can enjoy a reasonably happy and a fairly secure existence. If, on the other hand, you are erratic and unreliable, swift disaster may—and probably will—fall upon them. The engineer on a railroad train may be informed by astronomers and poets that he is much smaller than the stars, and much less permanent than the grass. But as far as the passengers on his train are concerned, he is more important than all the constellations that ever shone and all the grass that ever grew. Or think what your friendship and your love mean to the people who are devoted to you. Surely you realize that if you dropped from sight, or even if you stopped caring about them, their whole world would go black.

> The night has a thousand eyes
> The day but one,
> Yet the light of a whole world dies
> When the sun is gone.
>
> The mind has a thousand eyes
> The heart but one,
> Yet the light of a whole life dies
> When love is done. [4]

[4] Francis W. Bourdillon, in *The Night Has a Thousand Eyes*. By permission of Little, Brown and Company.

You are insignificant, valueless? Not so long as there is one person who loves you, and who craves your love in return.

Here is still a third fact all of us would do well to recall. Insignificant and temporary though we seem, we still have the power to cast influences far into the future and affect profoundly the course of coming events. We have this power because we are surrounded by human beings who have the unique abilities we have been discussing—the power to think, to create, to influence and be influenced by others, and to love. If you and I lived on Robinson Crusoe's island, surrounded only by sticks and stones, trees and the ocean, we might well ask despairingly, "What difference does it make *what* I do?" But we are not living on Robinson Crusoe's island. We are living in a world filled with infinitely sensitive, infinitely responsive human beings. Through them and their children we fling influences far down the years, and alter profoundly the direction of the world's development. Whether we realize it or not, we have the power to shape and determine the future.

Two generations ago a relatively unknown English clergyman was struck down by tuberculosis. For years he had been working in the slums of London, and now privation and overstrain had taken their heavy toll. Some friends moved him to a village in Devonshire where both he and they knew he would presently meet Death. Every morning the sick man lifted himself laboriously in his bed and watched the sun creep up the eastern sky. Would that be his last day? One morning the nurse found him dead in bed, his face turned peacefully toward that eastern window. On a nearby table lay a sheet of paper covered with feeble and almost illegible writing. The nurse deciphered a few words—"Heaven's morning breaks," "Earth's vain shadows flee." Then she gave the paper to the minister's friends, and thanks to their acquaintance with his handwriting they were able to make out the hymn he had written just before Death came.

> Abide with me, fast falls the eventide,
> The darkness deepens—Lord, with me abide!
> When other helpers fail and comforts flee
> Help of the helpless, O abide with me!

Since 1847 millions of people have sung Henry Francis Lyte's hymn. For generations to come other millions will sing it. From its brave words unnumbered men and women have gained, and will gain, new courage and new hope. Human beings insignificant and valueless? Think again, poet and astronomer, think again!

III

Once we understand the Christian belief in the supreme importance of human beings, and once we appreciate the basis in reason on which it rests, we can gain a firm confidence in the theory of life's meaning and purpose which liberal Protestantism is now offering the world. It is around the conviction that human life, even in its lowliest and least impressive forms, is the most valuable thing in our entire universe, that this theory is built. When we find ourselves compelled to face a hard and often tragic life this theory will give us courage to continue our struggle, sure that the battle is worth fighting and that the gains won in the battle will be permanent. What now is this modern theory of the meaning and purpose of life?

We Liberals are convinced that there is, at the heart of things, a Creative Mind and Power and Goodness to which we give the old name God. We believe in God's reality, though none of us has ever had direct sense-evidence of His presence, because the order and the adjustment apparent in Nature force us to conclude there is, somewhere behind the life-process, an Organizing Intelligence. What do we think God was planning when, uncounted centuries ago, He set in motion the growth-process which finally brought into existence our Earth and the living forms now evident upon it? We believe that His aim was to call into being human creatures who would possess the ability to grow in character—in intelligence, skill, and kindness. It was for this end that God initiated the vast evolutionary process. It is around human life and the development of human character that all history centers.

With this theory as a clue we can discover the meaning of the three great stages through which the evolutionary process has obviously passed. The first began when, as the astronomers now tell us, a mass of gas broke away from the parent Sun and then slowly liquefied in the cold of stellar Space. On that liquid a crust eventually formed, and after millions of years the solid, inert Earth came into being. The second stage of the evolutionary process began when on that lifeless Earth the first seeds of life made their appearance. Where they came from we cannot say. How and when they came we do not know. All we are sure of is that they did come, and that once here they flowered into innumerable forms. Then began the third stage through which the evolutionary process has passed, the stage in which we still find ourselves today. Above the highest level of the animal world appeared a creature with powers far greater and far more significant than those of any of his predecessors. That new creature was Man. Where he came from, how he came, and when he came we cannot say. All we know is that he did come, and that he inherited from the animal world the body and the brain which had been so slowly developed and so ingeniously perfected. With his appearance the development God had sought from the beginning —the development of human character—could at last begin.

What was the power which would force this development to take place? What was the spur which would drive human beings to win intelligence, gain skill, learn kindness? This incentive toward character-development was provided by the environment itself. Primitive men found themselves in a world which forced them to use their higher powers or suffer cruelly. It was the very fury of the storm which made them think and plan, and finally devise ingenious shelters for themselves and their children. It was the ever-present threat of pain and death which made them study and experiment, and finally begin to learn the secrets of medicine. And the development of kindness? Primitive men found themselves confronted not only by the relentless powers of Nature but also by the strength and the skill—sometimes the hostile strength and skill—of other human beings. If primitive men were to escape conflict and suffering they had to learn justice and kindness, tolerance and coöperation. The rule life laid down then, and still lays down today, is harsh and relentless yet singularly wise. "Grow in character, or perish. Learn wisdom and skill and kindness, or die." Under the stimulus of that rigorous alternative humanity has moved forward from the rough life of primitive society to the wiser, kinder, more skilful life of today. Under the continuing stimulus of that alternative humanity will, in the long centuries before us, move still further onward.

Why will this advance take place? Because suffering and disaster are the penalty if the advance is not made. How long will this racial progress continue? No one has the slightest idea. But with millions of years of growth behind us, with the propulsive forces quite as powerful now as they were in the past, and with man's understanding of the life-process and its demands growing ever clearer, the likelihood is that the advances to be made in the future will be even more extensive and significant than those made in the past. A world without disease, without poverty, without ignorance, without injustice, and without war seems—in the light of the gains already recorded —actually within our reach.

What about the individual human beings who inevitably perish as the race continues this long, slow advance? We Christians are convinced that the vast growth-process, of which we are both a product and a part, inevitably affects individuals as well as humanity as a whole. We believe that the divine purpose—the development of character—includes each one of us as well as our race. Thus we think that the incident of physical dissolution which we call death is in reality an insignificant episode, and that on the other side of this inevitable incident every human personality will continue its endless evolution. Where and under what circumstances that further growth will take place we cannot say. How it will take place, and what the relationship is between the evolving selves on that side of death and those on this side, we do not pretend to explain. But we are convinced that life and love, struggle and development, will continue; that they will continue for every human being; that they will continue indefinitely; and that the next phase of our evolution in character will begin at the precise point at which the present phase will leave off. Thus, according to our belief, the human race moves forward along the horizontal line we call the development of racial character, while each individual moves upward along the vertical line we call the development of individual character. There is no such thing as extinction, for either the race or the individual. Both are surrounded by the life, the love, the purpose of God; and both move onward toward the goal He established long before He set the evolutionary process in motion. It is the goal of a deeper and deeper knowledge, a greater and greater skill, a wider and wider kindness. Why can we face life, no matter how tragic life may prove, with courage and hope?

Because life has meaning, purpose, potential splendor. Life is our chance to start that growth in character which God has purposed for us. Why can we face death, no matter how cruel it may seem, inwardly undisturbed? Because death is merely an instant of apparent defeat in an eternity of brave advance.

> Do not fear
> And do not grieve for me,
> I shall not die!
> I am like the forest oak
> Which many suns have seasoned:
> My body will be a little heap of ashes
> Upon a hearth,
> But my soul will rise in flames
> That leap and soar
> And seek the stars.
> Do not fear
> And do not weep, my dear,
> When Death stoops to light the fire.[5]

IV

All this suggests the modern answer to a question which for centuries has puzzled thoughtful people. Does God have a plan for each individual? If He

[5] See "Release," by Jean G. Paxton, in *Quotable Poems*, vol. II, p. 259, Willett, Clark & Co.

does, why do so many disasters overtake the men and women who try to do their best?

The early Protestants believed that God does have a plan for each individual, but they pictured that plan in terms of a rigid and a detailed predestination. They maintained that, from the very beginning of Time, God had foreordained literally everything. They were convinced He had foreordained not only events but also the attitudes each individual would assume when the successive incidents in the chain of prearranged experiences took place. Why some people encounter an excessive number of disasters in their chain of experiences the early Protestants found it difficult to explain. All they could say was that the chain had been formed in its existing pattern "for the glory of God," and that as God wanted some people to die in ignorance and sin so He wanted others to live in hardship and suffering.

Today such beliefs have almost completely vanished. They persist only in shadowy and uncertain form—in the occasional statement that "whatever happens is God's will," and in the fast-fading belief that we should accept whatever comes to us as the deliberate, and ultimately beneficial, act of God.

Today, as modern science and modern religion combine to give us a new picture of the world and a new interpretation of life's meaning, a new theory of the divine plan for individuals is taking shape. We are now convinced that God has essentially the same plan for every human being—that each one of us should grow in character, and that each one of us should help those about him achieve this same growth. It was for this purpose that God put us all into life, and for this purpose that He forces us to live side by side in a world full of risks but also full of opportunities for the development of our finer powers. We cannot think that God superintends each trivial event, or that He deliberately maneuvers one person into one place and another into another. We certainly cannot believe that He is responsible for the tragic coincidences which, sooner or later, overwhelm us all. Rather we believe that God exposes us all to the harsh but effective schooling which life in such a world as ours provides, and then leads us all onward to the further schooling offered by another existence in another world. Out of this long and varied education the same gain will ultimately accrue to us all—growth in character. There is God's plan for individuals. Not a detailed and often cruel pre-destination. Rather a wise and kindly, though often rigorous, schooling. Its objective is not a static salvation for a few. Rather it is an ever-continuing development of intelligence, skill, and kindness for us all.

> Rebellious heart in the grip of Fate,
> Have patience, wait!
> Calm you, and hark to the great wind's blowing,
> Bearing seed to your hands for sowing . . .
> Drive deep the plow of sorrow and pain,
> Turn up rich soil for the later grain,
> Spare not the tears: they are needed as rain.
> Too long, too long has the field lain fallow,
> Now well prepared, and no longer shallow—
> Please God, a soul is growing! [*]

[*] See "Soul Growth," by Annerika Fries, in *Quotable Poems*, vol. II, p. 322, Willett, Clark & Co.

CHAPTER II

BREAKING THE GRIP OF WORRY

I

ON the evening of March 3, 1843 a middle-aged inventor was sitting in the gallery of the Senate Chamber in Washington. His name was Samuel F. B. Morse, and for the preceding eleven years he had been working on a strange device he called a telegraph. He was convinced it would be of great practical value, but in order to demonstrate that value he had to have an experimental telegraph line of considerable length. His own funds were exhausted, and two of his friends in Congress were trying to secure a federal appropriation of $30,000 with which to build this line. Unfortunately the session of Congress terminated that evening at midnight, and if the appropriation were not granted before that time the prospects for both the invention and the inventor were dark indeed. Morse was then fifty-two years of age, and he had less than one dollar to his name. What could the future hold for such a man?

As midnight approached, Morse sent an anxious message to his friends asking what the outlook was. They replied there was little time left before adjournment, that there were many bills still to be considered, and that Morse had better brace himself for a severe disappointment. On receiving this disheartening word, Morse gave up in despair and trudged wearily to his lodgings. Fifty-two years old, the work of eleven years wasted, and less than one dollar left. What would happen to him? Certainly he had every right to lie awake the rest of the night worrying over the future. But fortunately Morse had learned how to master fear. Writing a few days later to a friend he said, "In that unhappy frame of mind I reached my room, and made all my arrangements for leaving Washington on the morrow. Then, knowing from long experience whence my help must come in hours of difficulty, I disposed of all my cares, dropped to sleep, and rested as quietly as a child." [1]

[1] See Henry S. Coffin, *What Is There in Religion?* pp. 53, 54, The Macmillan Co.

There spoke a man who had broken the grip of worry.

Why does the average person lack this power? Why is control over anxiety such a problem for most of us? Our racial background suggests the answer. The jungle world of long ago, the world in which our animal ancestors lived for centuries, was filled with peril. An animal might fall from a tree and injure himself fearfully. He might make the mistake of creeping into an apparently empty cave, and there fall victim to the beast lurking in the darkness. He might fail to run from a forest fire, and then die a cruel death as the marching flames closed in about him. These were the perils of the jungle world, and any animal who failed to fear them and shun them soon paid for his carelessness with his life. Thus only those creatures that possessed a definite amount of caution, apprehensiveness, and dread of the unknown survived. These creatures passed on to their descendants these peculiar traits, and in the course of time they were bred deep into animal, subhuman, and finally human life. They are the source of our habit of worry today. In its original and uncontrolled form the instinctive dread of the unknown appears clearly in the animals we have domesticated. A horse shies from a fluttering newspaper, a dog backs away from a bonfire, and a kitten taken into a strange house scurries anxiously from room to room and finally hides under a piece of furniture. To one who seeks to understand the mechanisms of human conduct the actions of these animals tell a significant story.

Unfortunately the human world gives this ancient impulse toward anxiety not only an unprecedented stimulus but also many new and extensive areas in which to express itself. Obviously human beings to-day have far more to worry about than their animal ancestors ever had. The animals might be involved in an accident, a battle with another beast, or an encounter with one of the stern forces of Nature; but how short their list of perils compared with ours! When we enumerate the dangers surrounding a modern man we soon realize what a marvel it is that any one of us survives till nightfall. Every breath we draw brings into our sensitive breathing-apparatus a bewildering array of germs, some of them terrifically malignant. Every journey we take, even on foot, exposes us to perils far more numerous than

those of a jungle. Who knows how treacherous the
next ice-covered pavement may be? Who knows
what the driver of an approaching automobile may
suddenly do? Every business or professional venture
we undertake is crammed with risks. Without the
slightest warning, and in spite of the greatest watch-
fulness on our part, we may suddenly lose our
money, our job, and our confidence in our own sagac-
ity. Meantime, thanks to the fact we have climbed
above the animal level and gained an interest in
other people, the problems and perils confronting
our friends add still more burdens to the array already weighing heavily on the mind. We worry
about other people, particularly about our children,
quite as much as we worry about ourselves. The
result of the entire situation is that the modern world
is filled with men and women who are the pitiful
victims of chronic anxiety. They are always worrying, and worrying with apparently good cause, over
something or someone. From one year's end to the
other they never wholly escape the shadow of fear.

How can we conquer such anxiety? How can we
free ourselves from the grip of worry? We may
never be able to duplicate the achievements of the

men who, like Morse, entirely emancipate themselves from fear. But we can win at least a partial victory over this ancient enemy; and the long record of human experience shows clearly the steps we must take as we attempt this venture.

II

We may well begin our effort by distinguishing between justified and unjustified anxieties. If you watch people carefully you will soon discover that those who are the chronic slaves of fear are those who permit themselves to worry over anything and everything, while those who gain a certain control over anxiety are those who habitually banish from the mind worries that are essentially fantastic and unfounded. The first group of people starts worrying on the slightest provocation: the second refuses to start worrying till there is something serious to worry about. One of our humorists has recently drawn up what he calls a "Worry Table." It suggests in amusing fashion this distinction between justified and unjustified anxieties. On studying his chronic fears this man found they fell into five fairly distinct classifications:

1. Worries about disasters which, as later events proved, never happened. About 40% of my anxieties.
2. Worries about decisions I had made in the past, decisions about which I could now of course do nothing. About 30% of my anxieties.
3. Worries about possible sickness and a possible nervous breakdown, neither of which materialized. About 12% of my anxieties.
4. Worries about my children and my friends, worries arising from the fact I forgot these people have an ordinary amount of common sense. About 10% of my anxieties.
5. Worries that have a real foundation. Possibly 8% of the total.

What, for this man, is the first step in the conquest of anxiety? It is to limit his worrying to the few perils in his fifth group. This simple act will eliminate 92% of his fears. Or, to figure the matter differently, it will leave him free from worry 92% of the time.

Suppose you decide to banish from your mind, by a resolute effort of the will, all unjustified anxieties. What are the worries you will thus eliminate? You will certainly abandon most of your anxieties about your own health. Your body and your nerves are far stronger, far more resourceful, far more trustworthy than you realize. If you stop thinking about them, stop watching them, stop asking them how they feel and whether they will do their work, you will find they will operate with surprising ease and effectiveness. For all of us health, not sickness, is the normal state. To it we tend to return the moment we cease blocking our return by chronic fear. To say this is not to disparage the work of physicians or surgeons. It is certainly not to espouse the theory that disease is imaginary, or the notion that medical treatment is unnecessary. It is merely to say what every reputable doctor is saying constantly—that the worst enemy of health is chronic fear, and that the best prescription which can be compounded contains large admixtures of confidence, courage, and resolute cheerfulness.

All of us will also do well to abandon most of our worries about our own children. In the majority of instances those worries, like worries about our own health, eventually prove groundless. If you will look back to your own childhood you will see how true this is. Twenty, thirty, forty years ago scores of elderly people were worrying incessantly about you. Some of them were whispering that your school record was singularly unpromising, and that there was grave question whether you would ever win a diploma from any academic institution. Others were saying you showed a fatal fondness for play, a disastrous inability to apply yourself to the work in hand; and were prophesying that when you met the rigorous competition of the adult world you would be a sorry disappointment to your family and to yourself. Still others—and this was the most apprehensive group of all—stared in undisguised amazement at the individual you intended to marry. How could such a marriage prove successful? Were you utterly blind to the obvious limitations of your proposed life-partner? The worries of an earlier generation—and how unfounded most of them have proved to be! Has it never occurred to you that your anxieties about your children are probably equally fantastic?

> Better never trouble Trouble
> Till Trouble troubles you,
> For you only make that Trouble
> Double-Trouble when you do.
> And that Trouble, like a bubble
> That you're worrying about,
> May be nothing but a zero
> With the rim . . . soon out.[2]

[2] See David Keppel in *The World's Famous Short Poems*, p. 378, Harper & Bros.

III

A second step in the conquest of worry is this. Whenever you face a difficult situation, and fear begins to get the better of you, give your emotions an outlet in action. This practice of "working off" worries has brought a significant deliverance to multitudes of hard-pressed, apprehensive people. Consider this incident, recently reported by Admiral Byrd.

The success of his first expedition to Little America depended on the ability of his party to reach the Antarctic region during the brief summer-period, establish a camp there before winter began, and then when the sun reappeared make a dash for the Pole. There were forty-two men in the expedition, and on February 22, 1929 the ship which had brought them and their equipment to the Antarctic sailed away northward through a slowly freezing sea. The party was thus left to its own resources, perched insecurely on an ice-sheet some 2,300 miles south of civilization. By the middle of April the sun would disappear entirely, and for the next four months the forty-two men would face the incredible cold, darkness, and peril of the long Antarctic night. Would any of them survive? Would they reach the Pole when the sun reappeared? Even if they did reach the Pole, and even if they did return safely to Little America, would the ship that had agreed to call for them put in appearance and take them back to civilization before another—and that time a fatal—winter set in? There were many things to worry about: how was worry conquered?

Admiral Byrd gives this suggestive account of his camp on the ice-sheet and of the daily routine he shrewdly arranged. "We looked about us at Little America—with its three tiny houses, the airplanes we hoped would take us to the Pole, and the three spidery wireless-masts which connected us with far-away civilization. Behind the three houses our crates and boxes lay in a shapeless pile, and the yellow heads of our gasoline drums emerged here and there through the snow. Pieces of brown tarpaulin showed where other supplies lay half-buried in the drifts. A line of brown and white tents ran through the center of our little settlement, and near-by were the crates for the dogs. East, north, and south stood the eternal ice-barrier, glowing with strange and swiftly-changing colors. The ship had gone, and now we had to depend on ourselves. So we all pitched in to make our little home firm and snug against the swiftly-approaching winter." [8] That final sentence gives the clue to the explorers' conquest of worry. It was incessant activity which effectively checkmated anxiety. It was work which provided a safe outlet for the dangerous emotion of fear.

Many of the men and women who are living in more conventional situations have learned to master their worries in similar fashion. Whenever they face an alarming crisis they promptly work off their fear by doing something. Learning that their best friend is in unexpected difficulties, they dissipate their anxiety by writing him a letter. Finding themselves confronted by a particularly complicated and threatening day, they conquer their apprehensions by planning in detail the successive moves they will make during the coming hours. Burdened by secret fears for the future they conquer their distress and regain their poise by the act of prayer.

[8] See Richard E. Byrd, *Little America,* pp. 148-150, G. P. Putnam's Sons, 1930.

> Lord, when on my bed I lie
> Sleepless, then to Thee I cry:
> Put my anxious thought on Thee
> And on Thy dear charity,
> Make my worried prayer . . . and then
> Turn myself to sleep again.[4]

How many of us have found that poem true!

IV

The third step in the conquest of worry is different in type. We take it when we remind ourselves that in every complex and hazardous situation unexpected and essentially unpredictable developments are likely —at any moment—to begin taking place. Sometimes, of course, these new developments complicate our problem still further. Sometimes, on the other hand, they bring a swift and happy solution of it. To forget the possibility that some such fortunate turn of events may occur, to imagine that because the worst may happen the worst is certain to happen—to do these things is to disregard some of the most evident facts in human experience. Sometimes, apart from anything we or our friends consciously attempt, our problems solve themselves.

[4] See John Oxenham, *Bees in Amber,* p. 21. Copyrighted by the American Tract Society.

At the beginning of this chapter we told the story of Samuel Morse, the inventor of the telegraph. Purposely we left the story unfinished. On learning from his friends in the Senate that there was little chance the appropriation he sought would be granted, he walked home in despair. The experimental telegraph line would never be built, and he himself would have to start life anew! But the next morning, as he was finishing an unhappy breakfast, someone brought astonishing news. Just after he had left the Senate Chamber, his bill had been lumped with several other similar bills and hastily passed. The money he needed was his, and he could start building his experimental telegraph line at once. Morse's experience has repeated itself a million times in human life. The job we confidently expected to lose remained ours after all. The financial disaster from which there seemed no possible escape vanished into thin air. The operation we dreaded, and from which our apprehensive friends assured us we would never recover, proved to be a relatively simple and a highly successful affair. This is not imagination. This is not exaggeration. This is not blind optimism. It is the sober record of centuries of actual experience.

Suppose, in the particular case in hand, such an external deliverance does *not* come. Suppose the federal appropriation is *not* voted just after the inventor has returned home. What then? Often the unexpected development in the situation is a development which takes place within our own life. The critical situation calls forth within us a new endurance, a new courage, a new physical strength, a new emotional poise. We ourselves change, and though there is no change in the external situation the emergence of new powers within us raises our strength to such a point that we find ourselves able to manage difficulties which had hitherto been unmanageable.

An experience recently reported by a British sea-captain may serve as an illustration. In 1923 a small British freighter, the *Trevassa,* sank during a hurricane on the Indian Ocean. When the ship went down, the nearest bit of land—Rodriguez Island—was some 1,700 miles distant. The stretch of water between the sinking ship and that far-away island was one of the loneliest and stormiest on the seven seas. With every expectation that all hands would perish, the forty-four men on the freighter clambered into the life-boats and pushed off. Three members of the crew were seriously ill at the time. As a matter of fact they had to be lifted from their bunks, carried on deck, and lowered into the lurching life-boats. But consider the testimony the captain gave when, three weeks later, he and his men reached Rodriguez Island after all. "Strange as it may seem, the three sick men survived the weeks of extreme hardship remarkably well. One of them had been suffering, while on the ship, from a discharging hip-bone. A few days after the ship went down, when we were battling for our lives on that stormy sea, his wound healed completely. He suffered no further pain from it until we reached land. Then, curiously enough, the wound broke out again. The other two sick men had been suffering from heavy colds when we were on shipboard. We thought they would be among the first to die; for we had very little food and water to give them, and for three weeks they were exposed day and night to the elements. But after two days in the life-boat they proceeded to get well, and took their turns regularly at the oars with the rest of us." Then the captain adds a sentence which all of us would do well to ponder deeply:

"Apparently the additional effort which the crisis itself demanded effected a cure." [5] You are facing what seems an unendurable situation? Remember the unpredictable element in life! The difficulties confronting you may suddenly scatter. You yourself may suddenly acquire new strength, new courage, new insight. However hazardous and hopeless your situation seems, you can face it with confidence and with hope.

v

This thought of the new resources which may disclose themselves within us gives the clue to one of the most important of the new beliefs now held by liberal Protestants. For centuries men fancied that the help God gives in our times of need is a sudden, miraculous, and infinitely gratifying change in the external situation. A storm may be stilled, a plague arrested, food and shelter dramatically provided. Dominated by this belief in external interferences, religiously-minded individuals collected incidents apparently bearing out their theory, and included them in their sacred books. Thus the Bible is filled

[5] See Cecil Foster, *1700 Miles in Open Boats*, pp. 67, 68, Houghton Mifflin Co., 1924.

with accounts of external interpositions wrought by God for the benefit of hard-pressed favorites. For centuries these miracle stories were the stock in trade of Christian preachers, and around them orthodox Christian teaching in reference to God's help and answers to prayer was built. Today liberal Protestants frankly question the truth of these old wonder-tales. We question them, not because we think it is impossible for God to bring such deliverances, but because the long record of human experience indicates that He does not give this type of help.

But does this mean we Liberals abandon faith in divine assistance? Nothing of the kind! It means that we look for the divine assistance in the world within rather than the world without. We are convinced that God helps us, not by altering our external situation, but by changing us; not by making our difficulties easier but by making us stronger. As we force ourselves to grow quiet and face our hard situations without fear, as we rally what resources of endurance and insight we already possess, what happens? The external situations remain exactly what they have always been, but we ourselves change. God releases within our own nature a strength and a resourcefulness we did not dream we possessed. He discloses within us a poise and a peace which the world can never give, and which all the tragedies in the world can never quite take away. This is God's help. This is His answer to our prayer.

CHAPTER III

BEING WILLING TO BE YOURSELF

I

HERE is a vivid poem by Theodosia Garrison. You will notice it describes three entirely different people, but that all three of them are facing the same inner problem.

> The gypsies passed her little gate
> She stopped her wheel to see:
> A brown-faced pair who walked the road
> Free as the wind is free.
> And suddenly her tidy room
> A prison seemed to be.
>
> Her shining plates against the walls,
> Her sunlit, sanded floor,
> The brass-bound wedding chest that held
> Her linen's snowy store,
> The very wheel whose humming died—
> Seemed only chains she bore.
>
> She watched the foot-free gypsies pass,
> She never knew or guessed

> The wistful dream that held them close,
> The longing in each breast—
> Some day to know a home like hers
> Wherein their hearts might rest.[1]

What is the problem pictured there so skilfully? A problem as old as history, and as universal as human life. It is the problem of being willing to be yourself.

Obviously this is a problem which concerns older rather than younger people. During our early years no one knows what abilities may lie hidden within us, or to what heights of achievement we may ultimately rise if our ambitions and our energies are adequately stimulated. Therefore the older people about us urge us to try our hand at anything and everything, and tell us if we will only work our hardest we may finally astonish everyone by the magnitude of our achievement. At such a time to urge youngsters to be willing to be themselves is to give them the worst possible advice. What they ought to do is try to be something other, something better, than they give promise of being. But when

[1] From *The Dreamers and Other Poems,* by Theodosia Garrison, copyright, 1917, by Doubleday, Doran & Company, Inc.

we reach the thirties, forties, and fifties our situation changes. Our life-work, whatever it happens to be, digs a channel within which the tide of our thoughts and our activities habitually flows. Our ever-enlarging array of responsibilities restricts sharply the range of our endeavors. Then emerges, slowly but inevitably, the problem we are now discussing—the problem of being willing to be yourself.

It is an open secret that many middle-aged and elderly people never succeed in solving this problem. Down to the day of their death they are never reconciled to the self life has given them, the career circumstance has charted out for them, the environment within which Fate forces them to live. Think, for example, of the men and women in middle-life who are unwilling to accept the fact they are growing old. To the secret amusement of all the bona-fide youngsters in the vicinity they try to talk young, act young, and (most disastrous of all) look young. On this single point—the number of their birthdays— they are not willing to be themselves. Or think of the individuals who are not willing to accept the one great disappointment life has thrust upon them. Year after year they tell their minister and their doctor that they were once defeated in a political campaign, that they were once tricked out of their savings by a dishonest relative, or that the child from whom they expected so much proved a lamentable failure. In this one area of their inner life rebellion always persists. Is all the restlessness in the world limited to such rigid, embittered personalities? Would that it were! Unfortunately even the best and bravest of us have days when we want to be anything but what we are, hours when we hate nothing so much as the career we must follow.

> The railroad track is miles away
>   And the day is loud with voices speaking,
> Yet there isn't a train goes by all day
>   But I hear its whistle shrieking.
>
> At night there isn't a train goes by,
>   Though the night is still for sleep and dreaming,
> But I see its cinders red on the sky
>   And hear its engine steaming.
>
> My heart is warm for the friends I make,
>   And better friends I'll not be knowing:
> Yet there isn't a train I wouldn't take
>   No matter where it's going! [2]

[2] From *Second April*, published by Harper & Bros. Copyright, 1921, by Edna St. Vincent Millay.

Is there any one of us who has not known that feeling?

How can we conquer such moods of restlessness and rebellion? How can we make ourselves willing, or at least not wholly unwilling, to be ourselves?

II

If we seek to conquer restlessness we may well begin our effort by studying our own life-pattern and noting its favorable elements. What do we mean by a life-pattern? We mean the precise combination of abilities and limitations, opportunities and restrictions, potential happinesses and potential disasters which forms the framework of a particular personality and a particular career. Obviously life-patterns differ with different people. Consider the three individuals in the poem we quoted at the beginning of this chapter. The young mother, sitting in her tiny room and gazing enviously at the gypsies, had a life-pattern entirely different from theirs. Circumstance had given her the great joy of home-making, and the still greater joy of motherhood. But circumstance also compelled her to spend her years in a small and rather dull community, and forced her to dedicate her life to a family that was often unappreciative and sometimes distinctly irritating. What a curious combination of light and shade in her life-pattern! The life-pattern of the gypsies was entirely different. They had the chance to enjoy perfect freedom and incessant journeying, but they also found on their shoulders an ever-growing burden of friendlessness, homelessness, and uncertainty about the future. How could these three individuals conquer restlessness? Each must study his own life-pattern, note its favorable elements, accept its unfavorable ones, and then not demand an impossible perfection in it. The young mother must note the joys of home-life, fasten her attention on them, accept the problems which home-life invariably brings, and then not expect to enjoy a settled existence and a wandering existence at the same time. The gypsies must take their specialized satisfactions, find the happinesses waiting there for them, and then not ask to be both gypsies and towns-folk simultaneously. To study one's own life-pattern, locate its opportunities and its delights, refuse to be distressed by its limitations, and then persistently live in the sunny area of one's own little world—here is the first step toward the conquest of chronic restlessness and the acquisition of abiding inward peace.

Suppose you take this first step. Can you find, in your involved and puzzling world, genuine and abiding happiness? All we can say is that thousands of other people have done this very thing. Some of these people, compelled to live in a village when they had always dreamed of living in a city, have accepted their disappointment cheerfully, have set out to make what friendships they could in their little world, and have finally discovered that their village is radiant with interest and affection. Some of these people, denied the supreme joys of marriage and parenthood, have accepted their restriction, have located another career, and have finally made themselves a blessing not to three or four children but to a thousand. And what shall we say of the men and women who, missing the undoubted satisfactions of financial success, have found in some form of artistic self-expression a joy which wealth can never give and poverty never take away? Edgar Lee Masters describes a man of this type in "Spoon River Anthology." Study the confession of Fiddler Jones, and note how much happiness he had found in his tiny, unimpressive career.

> The Earth keeps some vibration going
> There in your heart, and that is you.
> How could I till my forty acres
> (Not to speak of getting more!)
> With a medley of horns, bassoons, and piccolos
> Stirred in my brain by crows and robins
> And the creak of a windmill?
> I never started to plow
> That someone did not stop in the road
> And take me away to a dance or a picnic.
> I ended up with my forty acres,
> I ended up with a broken fiddle,
> And a broken laugh, and a thousand memories—
> And not a single regret! [3]

III

Another thing we must do if we seek to conquer restlessness is learn to manage our memories. As the years pass, life gives each one of us a motley array of recollections—some of them infinitely happy and some infinitely sad. On our ability to manage those memories—keep the tragic ones out of sight,

[3] From *Spoon River Anthology* by Edgar Lee Masters (Macmillan). By permission of the author.

and hold the radiant ones in the center of our attention—depends to a surprising extent our ability to achieve contentment. Some years ago a woman who had become an invalid at an early age sent me this revealing letter. Notice how completely she had mastered restlessness, and notice too the secret of her achievement. "I shall be thirty-one years old next Sunday, and I am sorry to say I am hopelessly crippled with arthritis. It is nearly a year since I was lifted from my bed, and nearly three years since I was able to take a step or use my hands in any way. Yet how much I have to be cheerful about! I have parents who do everything for me, a fine room in which to live, and friends who are constantly bringing me happiness. Before the arthritis developed I was a school-teacher. What do you think the children in my school have just done? They have raised some money and bought me a fine radio. That gift and the affection behind it are a wonderful joy to me." In that young woman's life were memories which might have driven her mad with grief, disappointment, protest, and inner conflict. But there were other memories that could fill even a prison-world like hers with radiance. How did she solve the problem of restlessness? How did she make herself willing to be what she had to be? By managing her memories.

How can you and I gain this ability? How can we control the thoughts which, for good or for ill, have such power over us? There is only one way—by careful, deliberate, long-continued practice. Fortunately any one of us who is willing to attempt this self-discipline can begin his effort at any time. A doctor once told me how to start. He said, "Picture a tiny closet in the furthest corner of your mind. There is a lock on the closet door, and you have the key. Whenever there emerges within your mind a thought which confuses you, angers you, or distresses you, take that thought and resolutely lock it inside that closet. Put there the recollections of the tragedy you have never been able to understand, the memories of your own embarrassing failures, the remembrance of other people's unkindnesses. Lock the door securely upon them all, and then bring into the focus of your attention the thoughts which create within you courage, confidence, and friendliness." You and I do not need to grow restless and cynical as we leave youth behind. We do not need to become bitter and rebellious as we become old. If we teach ourselves to manage our memories we can make the last years of life, however puzzling and disappointing they may prove, some of our bravest and our best.

> God keep my heart attuned to laughter
>   When youth is done,
> When all the days are gray days, coming after
>   The warmth, the sun.
> God keep me then from bitterness, from grieving,
>   When life seems cold:
> God keep me loving and believing
>   As I grow old.[4]

IV

There is one other self-discipline which we must undertake if we seek to conquer restlessness. We must remind ourselves frequently that there are two entirely different types of achievement—direct and indirect. Direct achievement is the obvious and the familiar type. A man organizes a successful business, discovers a cure for disease, or taking the lead in a much-needed movement for reform finally cre-

---

[4] Author unknown. See *Quotable Poems,* vol. II, p. 240, Willett, Clark & Co., 1931.

ates new social or political institutions. His ultimate accomplishment is spectacular and unmistakable, and the credit for it obviously belongs to him alone. This is direct achievement, and it is for direct achievement that most of us secretly yearn.

But there is of course another, and an essentially different, type of achievement. Here is a man who finds in his community organizations and institutions which are always working to strengthen the finer elements in the community's life. He does his best to support these institutions, and through them he makes his contribution—large or small—to the building of a better world. No one can show a connection between the little he does today and the ultimate victory these organizations finally gain. But there is such a connection, and through these organizations this inconspicuous and soon-forgotten individual attains a significant though admittedly indirect achievement. Or here is another man who finds himself surrounded by individuals, old or young, who deeply need the incentive and the help he can give them. Without encouragement and assistance from him they face almost certain defeat: with his aid they have at least a chance of winning their long, hard battle. Year after year this man gives his best to these needy neighbors. Ultimately some of them, thanks to his assistance, gain a glorious triumph. No one can ever chart the precise connection between their final success and the aid he gave them, perhaps unconsciously, years before. No one can ever determine how large a proportion of their attainment is due to his activity in their behalf. Yet everyone who understands the complex interrelationships between human lives realizes that through the success of these other people this man has won his own victory in life. Here again is indirect achievement.

During the World War a small boy in one of our American cities was compelled to undergo a serious and wholly unexpected operation. It happened that he had an older brother who was serving with the American troops in France, a brother to whom he was ardently devoted. Just before the older brother had left for the front, he had given the younger brother several mementos, and it was one of these mementos that the small boy insisted on taking to the hospital with him. As he was wheeled into the operating room the nurse noticed he was holding something in his tiny first. She held out her hand quietly and said, "Let me keep it for you. I'll have it right here when you come out of the ether." But the little fellow shook his head. "No," he said, "I want it myself. It's going to help me a lot. It's a button from the coat of a real soldier." How much help that elder brother, stationed in far-away France, was giving that younger brother, lying in a hospital in America! There was indirect achievement.

It is the thought of these obscure and often-unrecognized accomplishments which has helped some of us keep our faith in God's use of our little lives. As we look back over our careers we see pitifully few evidences of direct achievement. As we look ahead we realize there is little chance we shall ever create a great institution, discover a profound truth, or initiate a significant social development. If direct achievements are the only achievements, then our lives have been evident failures; and God's use of our tiny best has been cruelly inadequate. But when we remember there are indirect as well as direct accomplishments, when we recall the fact that through institutions and through other people we can work ultimate and significant changes within life, then our confidence in ourselves and our faith in God's use of us come streaming back into our hearts. The ultimate source of restlessness in many lives is a secret sense of failure. The cure for that sense of failure and the feeling of restlessness which it breeds is a new understanding of indirect achievement, a new glimpse of the secret ways in which God uses us when we do our best.

> A narrow window may let in the light,
> A tiny star dispel the gloom of night,
> A little deed an ancient wrong set right.
>
> One look, and there may be an end to strife;
> One smile, and Hate may sheathe her cruel knife,
> One word, but it may be God's word of life! [5]

[5] Florence Earle Coates, in *Quotable Poems*, vol. II, p. 230, Willett, Clark & Co., 1931.

CHAPTER IV

THE SECRET OF GETTING A LOT DONE

I

SOME time ago an English poet published an unusual verse entitled "The Sleepers." The idea for it came to him when, early one morning, he was walking along the Thames Embankment in London.

> As I walked down the waterside
> This morning in the cold, damp air,
> I saw a hundred women and men
> Huddled in rags, and sleeping there.
> These people have no work, thought I,
> And long before their time they die.
>
> That moment on the waterside
> A lighted car came at a bound,
> I looked inside and saw a score
> Of pale and weary men who frowned;
> Each man sat in a huddled heap,
> Carried to work while fast asleep.
>
> Ten cars rushed down the waterside,
> Like lighted coffins in the dark,

> With twenty dead men in each car
> Who must be brought alive by work.
> These people work too hard, thought I,
> And long before their time they die.[1]

This contrast between underworked and overworked individuals is of course not limited to the lower strata of society. At every level, all the way to the top of the scale, we find the same two groups —the first composed of those who have too little to do, the second composed of those who have too much. Consider the verse this English poet might have written had he visited the aristocratic sections of London rather than the dismal area along the Thames. In that other poem his first stanza would have described well-to-do men and women who had no serious responsibilities, and his second their neighbors—public officials, business executives, professional men—who were breaking down from overstrain. Why are there, everywhere in society, these contrasting groups? Partly because society is poorly organized. Partly because chance plays a significant rôle in human affairs. But mainly because human beings differ—in ability, in ambition, in responsive-

---

[1] From *Songs of Joy* by W. H. Davies. By permission of Jonathan Cape, Ltd.

ness to the needs of others. No matter how much we finally do to eliminate unemployment and overstrain, there will always be some individuals with too light a burden and some with one that is far too heavy. The underworked and the overworked—both types are with us today, and in all probability both will be with us indefinitely in the future.

Suppose now you belong to the overworked group. Suppose that, no matter how persistently you try to dodge extra burdens and avoid surplus responsibilities, they perversely converge upon you. How can you manage your double load? What is the secret of getting a lot done?

II

Part of the secret is obvious to everyone. If we want to accomplish more than the average person does we must utilize for work the fragments of time the average person wastes. Some years ago the girls in one of the New England colleges complained that too much work was assigned them, that there were not enough hours in the day to complete their required tasks. The faculty thereupon proposed that a careful study be made of the way in which the average girl in the college was using her time. Fifty students, representing many different types and groups, were asked to keep for two weeks a detailed and an exact record of their occupations. These records were then combined and averaged, and the results of the study published—without faculty comment—in the undergraduate weekly. It was found that the average girl in the college, after making due allowance for the necessities of eating, sleeping, dressing, attending classes, and spending a reasonable amount of time on other essentials, had each week 45½ hours of free time. What use did she make of this time? Some 19 hours she used wisely and effectively—in athletics, in outdoor exercise, in college activities, in reading, and in attendance at the services in the college chapel. But what happened to the rest of her free time, 26½ hours each week?

According to the average of the fifty separate records, those hours were spent as follows:

1½ hours at a local tea-room
1½ hours playing bridge
2   hours at parties
2½ hours at the theater or the movies
2½ hours dancing
12½ hours talking

4 hours—the balance of the time—vanished completely.

We all agree that all work and no play make Jack a dull boy, and Jack's sister an extremely unattractive girl. But if Jack and his sister are really in earnest about getting a lot done, is it not fairly evident where they should begin their effort?

A century ago a young man named Thomas B. Macaulay, employed full time in a responsible position in the British War Office, decided there were probably spare moments which he could profitably use writing verses. In 1842 he published a volume of poems entitled "Lays of Ancient Rome," a volume which the world has been admiring ever since. Every poem in the book was written "after hours." Some years later a Prime Minister of England decided there were probably spare moments in the busy life of a Prime Minister, and thereupon he began locating those moments and using them in writing a novel. The novel was finally finished in 1880 when the author, Benjamin Disraeli, was seventy-six years old. An English publisher valued the manuscript so highly that he paid Disraeli a cool $50,000 for it. Or turn to our own land. Two generations ago a young man named John Fiske was studying at Harvard. He spent his summer vacations at Middletown, Connecticut; and each summer— after reserving a reasonable amount of time for recreation, outdoor exercise, and complete mental rest— he carefully saved the remaining moments for serious study. Here is a paragraph from a letter he wrote a friend at the beginning of one of these summer vacations. "I have brought with me to Middletown for my summer reading the Old Testament in the original Hebrew, together with several German commentaries. I also have here a book on Hebrew syntax, a volume on Sanskrit inflections, and several other profitable works of a similar nature. Just for variety I have also brought along Dante in the original Italian, and a textbook on zoölogy." [2] The secret of getting a lot done? Part of that secret is surely evident to us all!

> If you can fill the unforgiving minute
> With sixty seconds' worth of distance run,
> Yours is the Earth, and everything that's in it,
> And what is more you'll be a man, my son! [3]

[2] See John S. Clarke, *John Fiske,* vol. I, p. 252. By permission of, and by arrangement with, Houghton Mifflin Co.

[3] Reprinted by permission of Mr. Rudyard Kipling from the poem entitled "If" in *Rewards and Fairies.* Copyright, 1910. Also by permission of Doubleday Doran & Company, publishers, and A. P. Watt & Son, agents.

III

But the more important half of the secret of accomplishment lies deeper. It lies in the inner life of the individual. Consider this significant statement, found in a current volume on applied psychology. "Our primary task is not to fit a man to face his environment, but to fit him to face himself. A man cannot meet the onslaughts of the outside world successfully unless he has first established harmony within his own soul. Only when he has settled the conflicts within himself is he ready to face his environment. With peace in his own heart he is, as the World War demonstrated, capable of surviving the most terrible ordeals. But without peace in his own heart he cannot face even the responsibility of writing an ordinary letter." [4] If you watch yourself carefully you will soon realize how true those words are. If a man permits confusion, strain, or turmoil to invade his inner life even the slightest burden soon becomes a crushing load. But if a man keeps himself free from inward conflicts and spiritual tensions he can, as multitudes of super-busy people demonstrate,

[4] See J. A. Hadfield, *Psychology and Morals,* p. 41, Robert M. McBride and Co., 1926.

work day in and day out, year in and year out, with amazing effectiveness and little or no sense of fatigue. As the psychologists are forever reminding us, it is internal strains rather than external burdens which exhaust us.

What now are some of the familiar inward tensions against which we must guard ourselves if we hope to enlarge our capacity for achievement? Or, to put the matter differently, how can we gain that inner quietness which is essential to better-than-average accomplishment?

We can begin gaining quietness by conquering self-pity. Many busy people, noting the fact that extra burdens are devolving upon them, and realizing that their associates are singularly free from surplus loads, instantly begin to feel sorry for themselves. They tell themselves, particularly at the end of a long and wearing day, that it is a pity they have so much to do, so many problems to solve, so many dependent individuals to help. If they could only dodge these extra burdens how much easier and happier life would be! How much more effectively they could handle the single job which would remain! What is the effect of this self-pity? Instantly and inevitably it creates a vicious sense of strain within the personality. That sense of strain in turn makes quiet, easy, frictionless accomplishment impossible. As long as we feel sorry for ourselves because we have so much to do, as long as we pity ourselves because we must carry more than a single share of life's burdens, just so long will the ability to do a more-than-average amount of work remain perversely beyond our reach. On the other hand, as soon as we banish self-pity—even self-pity in this somewhat justifiable form—the sense of protest and strain will begin to fade from our inner life, and the power to work long and hard will emerge within us.

How can we conquer this form of self-pity? How can we make ourselves glad rather than sorry that we have a great deal to do? Many people have won this victory by the simple expedient of reminding themselves that their numerous burdens and their multiplied responsibilities are in reality an asset rather than a liability. When all is said, it is our hardships which create resourcefulness of mind and courage of spirit. It is our problems which give us insight and judgment. It is our burdens which bring us an ultimate strength. We must not regard a double load as a handicap. If we learn to carry it in the right way, if we learn to let it develop within us the powers which it can develop, it may finally prove our greatest blessing.

> I love the friendly faces of old sorrows,
> They have no secrets that I do not know;
> They are so old I think they have forgotten
> What bitter words were spoken long ago.
> I hate the cold, stern faces of new sorrows
> That wait and watch, and catch me all alone;
> I should be braver if I could remember
> How friendly all the older ones have grown! [5]

Those familiar lines apply not only to the sorrows we call disappointments and tragedies. They also apply to the sorrows we call extra burdens and surplus responsibilities.

IV

As we seek inward quietness and through it the power to achieve, we shall also do well to disregard irresponsible comment and unfair criticism. Notice the conditioning adjectives. Some of the comments and criticisms passed upon us should prove of the

[5] Karle W. Baker, in *Burning Bush*, p. 26, Yale University Press, 1922.

utmost value. The comments made by those who know us and our problems, and who have our best interests at heart, should show us where and how we can improve our way of working and our method of meeting and managing people. The criticisms made by those who are familiar with the technical difficulties of our particular task, and who are beyond any suspicion of envy or malice, should tell us what our weak points are and what we can do to eliminate them. To turn a deaf ear to such comments and to reject angrily such criticisms, is to sentence ourselves to an unimproved and unimprovable future.

But unfortunately only part of the comments and criticisms which reach us are of this discriminating and constructive type. The rest, as experience soon shows, are of inferior quality and insignificant value. Most of us are surrounded by individuals who are sensitive, quick-spoken, and sometimes secretly envious. Such men and women are almost certain to pass unfair comments on us, and make cruelly undiscerning criticisms of us. The more successful our efforts become, the more bitter such comments and criticisms are apt to grow. If we let ourselves be disturbed by the gibes and the denunciations of these incompetent individuals, particularly when their remarks are quoted by third parties whose sincerity is questionable, we betray ourselves into a wholly needless distress of mind. As we seek to gain that quietness of spirit which is so essential to better-than-average achievement we must teach ourselves, at any cost in self-discipline, to disregard the comments, the criticisms, the generalized abuse, and the specialized indictments of those who are not competent to pass judgment upon us, and of those whose disinterestedness and friendliness are patently open to question. Out of long and painful experience Abraham Lincoln wrote five sentences which all of us, particularly those who are in public life, would do well to study. "If I tried to read, much less answer, all the criticisms made of me and all the attacks leveled against me, this office would have to be closed for all other business. I do the best I know how, the very best I can. I mean to keep on doing this, down to the very end. If the end brings me out all wrong, then ten angels swearing I had been right would make no difference. If the end brings me out all right, then what is said against me now will not amount to anything."

How can we achieve such serenity of spirit? How can we lift ourselves above the level on which cruel comments hurt, and on which unjustified criticisms fester in the mind? There is only one way. We must brace ourselves in advance for a certain amount of misunderstanding and hostility, and a much larger amount of indifference and unresponsiveness. Then, when superficial comments and irresponsible criticisms descend upon us, we must let them slip off the surface of our mind as raindrops slide down a windowpane—leaving not a trace behind. Expecting a certain amount of misunderstanding, we shall be neither surprised nor disturbed when it comes. Realizing in advance we shall never satisfy everyone, we shall be able to remain inwardly undisturbed when we find there are some individuals who do not enthuse over us, and others who are definitely hostile toward us.

You may get through the world but your march will
    be slow
If you listen to all that is said as you go;
You'll be worried and troubled and kept in a stew
For talkative folks must have something to do
    And so they will talk.

If you're quiet and modest it will be presumed
That your humble position is slyly assumed;
You're a wolf in sheep's clothing, or just a plain fool,
But don't get excited, keep perfectly cool,
    And let people talk.

If you show resolution and boldness of heart,
A slight inclination to take your own part,
Some people will say you're conceited and vain,
But keep right on working and never explain,
    For folks will still talk.

The best rule to follow is: Do as you please.
Then your mind will be quiet, your spirit at ease.
We all can be sure of some praise, some abuse:
Don't listen for comments, it's a plan not to use,
    For people will talk.[6]

V

We shall also do well, as we seek inward quietness
and through it the power to achieve, to arrange our
tasks in such a way that we shall invariably be ahead
of our work rather than behind it. Why is such an
arrangement of our burdens helpful? Because an
uncompleted task invariably creates within the mind

[6] Samuel Dodge, in *The World's Famous Short Poems*, p. 65,
Harper & Bros.

a highly disturbing sense of strain. By keeping ahead of our work we can eliminate this element of friction, and increase proportionately our capacity for smooth, unwearied accomplishment.

Perhaps two illustrations will make the point clear. Here is a man who, in the midst of an important piece of work, receives an urgent invitation to drop everything and join in a game of golf. After some hesitation he decides to leave his work, finish it at a later time, and enjoy the delightful foursome which has been promised. But when he reaches the first tee and attempts to make a good drive he discovers that something distressing has happened. His driver and the ball do not connect, and the further he goes on the course the more colossal his score becomes. Or here is a mother who must write her daughter a long and important letter. Half way through the undertaking she decides to postpone finishing the task. She will go to bed, enjoy a sound sleep, and the next day write more tactfully. But though she goes to bed she cannot go to sleep: all night long she has moments of semi-consciousness in which the blurred thought of the letter emerges persistently before her mind. What has happened to these two persons? In each case an unfinished task, an unfulfilled but pressing responsibility, reaches down from the past to disturb and perplex the present. The handicap against which each of these individuals is struggling appears, in less obvious form, in the life of every person who is behind in his work and who is trying wearily to catch up. Against the inward friction which unfinished tasks invariably create he struggles painfully and helplessly, usually unaware of the true—and needless—source of his difficulties.

How can we correct such a situation? We must do what thousands of other people have done—scheme and struggle until, after a day or a week or a month of intense effort, we come abreast of our responsibilities and then forge at least a few steps ahead of them. The further ahead we move, the easier the task of keeping ahead becomes. It becomes easier for the simple reason that the source of our previous sense of strain is removed. You say you have so much to do, and that you are already so far behind in your work, that it is impossible for you to catch up with your tasks? But other people, far more heavily burdened than you are, have caught up with their responsibilities. Why not shut yourself in with your work for a day or even a week, dodge all new duties, and at last push yourself abreast of your tasks? During the Coolidge régime in Washington a visitor called at the White House and, armed with a special card of admission, gained entrance to the President's private study. He expected to find Mr. Coolidge hidden behind a desk piled high with unread documents, unsigned letters, and unfinished business. Instead he saw a flat-topped table with not a paper in sight, and found Mr. Coolidge standing quietly by the window. Lots to do, of course; but Mr. Coolidge had learned to keep ahead of his work. By doing so he dodged completely the strain which unfulfilled responsibilities inevitably create within the mind.

VI

But the most important discipline of all is yet to be mentioned. If you and I seek inward quietness, and through it the power to achieve, we must rid ourselves of secret fear. What is the thing busy people are usually afraid of? It is not Death. Busy people have too much to do here and now to consider the far future. Neither are busy people—in most instances —afraid of an ultimate breakdown. The very pressure of their work keeps them thinking of their present duties rather than their future physical condition. The thing most busy people are afraid of is, curiously enough, themselves. Can they meet the heavy demands that are being made upon them? Have they enough physical strength to manage the long day, enough mental and emotional resilience to keep at their best amid swiftly changing situations, enough control of their nerves to relax and drop to sleep when night finally comes? When they have so much to do, and so many different things to do, is there power enough within them to get everything done and done well? These are the secret questions which perplex busy people. The thing most of them fear is themselves.

How can we conquer such self-distrust? By recalling the amazing endurance of other people, and by reminding ourselves that what others are doing— and doing under circumstances far more difficult than ours—we too can do. Time and again this simple effort will free us from anxiety about ourselves, and send us forward into a busy day with confidence and anticipation rather than apprehensiveness and self-distrust.

Some years ago the captain of a Pacific liner told me the almost incredible story of a stowaway who, hiding on that vessel, had succeeded in making the long voyage from Australia to Canada. On the top deck of the liner were sixteen life-boats, each stocked with a meager supply of water, chocolate, crackers, and condensed milk. The law provides that at the conclusion of each round-trip between Canada and Australia the life-boats must be thoroughly examined and the emergency rations renewed. At the end of a certain voyage, when the ship was lying at her pier in Vancouver, the sailors who were doing this work discovered that someone had been living inside one of the life-boats during the northward trip. The keg of water had been broken open, and the stores of food completely consumed. The bottom of the boat was littered with cigarette butts, and several articles of badly soiled clothing were lying there. In the boat the sailors eventually found a calendar with certain days carefully checked, and the discharge papers someone had secured from a Danish vessel which had docked in Sydney, Australia, several weeks before. Bit by bit, as in a detective story, the officers of the liner pieced together an almost incredible story of shrewdness, courage, and sheer endurance. The story was this.

A Danish sailing-vessel had reached Sydney, left her cargo, and discharged some members of her crew. One of the sailors who thus found himself jobless determined to make his way to Canada. On a Saturday night he crept aboard this Canadian liner, made his way to the top deck, removed the tight-fitting canvas cover from one of the life-boats, and crept inside. With him he carried a change of clothing, a supply of cigarettes, and a calendar. As each day passed, he made a mark on his calendar and thus kept an accurate record of the passage of time. The Wednesday after he concealed himself in the life-boat the liner sailed for Vancouver. The voyage lasted twenty-two days, and took the ship across the Equator. The heat within that covered life-boat, hung directly against the sun, must have been terrific, and the demands on the imprisoned sailor's endurance must have been almost intolerable. Undoubtedly he made, in the dead of night, occasional sallies from his hiding-place, and undoubtedly he lifted a corner of the cover on the seaward side of the life-boat when the heat within became unendurable. But hour after hour he resolutely huddled there, and each night he checked off another day on his crumpled calendar. Finally the ship reached Vancouver, and that night the stowaway slipped ashore. He had inadvertently left his discharge papers and his calendar in the lifeboat, grim evidences of a victory won against appalling odds.

You are afraid of yourself? You think you cannot manage the strains coming upon you? Look at other people—busier than you are, older than you are, more burdened than you are. They are mastering life. They are getting their work done. You can win victory too.

CHAPTER V

MANAGING PERSONAL ANTAGONISMS

I

SOME time ago I received this letter from a stranger in the Middle West. He had read one of my books, and here are his rather violent comments upon it. "I want to tell you that you and all the other ministers in Christendom are wolves in sheep's clothing. You and Fosdick and Billy Sunday and Father Coughlin and Mrs. McPherson are all working a racket. In your palatial churches are amusements comparable to Coney Island, and dance-halls which would be meaningless were it not for the presence there of the opposite sex. Like Satan, the father of lies, you say to people, 'Surely ye shall not die!' But you will have your reward—defeat, dissolution, disorganization, and scatterment. You say people to-day do not worship idols? But how about automobiles, airplanes, and tall buildings? How about Science and Modernism? You know well enough that people are now claiming they can meet the exigencies of the future with the NRA, with Buy Now Campaigns, and with the reform of the Churches. But all these things are the death-throes of the Two Great Harlots—False Religion and Commercialism. All you ministers are Prophets of Baal, Harpies, and Pharaoh's Chickens."

Are clergymen the only people who encounter such hostility? Certainly not! Every man in public life encounters it. Consider the situation of the average doctor. If his patients fail to recover, or if they recover less rapidly and less completely than their relatives anticipated, the physician in charge of the case is almost certain to be roundly condemned. Why did he not prescribe a different treatment? Why did he not admit his incompetence and summon other physicians for consultation? Or consider the predicament of bankers, brokers, and financial advisers. If a banker, striving to protect the funds entrusted to him by depositors, refuses to dispense loans with lavish hand, he is certain to be denounced by would-be borrowers as hard-fisted, greedy, and totally lacking in public spirit. If the investments recommended by a broker or a financial adviser prove less remunerative than investors anticipated, investors can usually be counted upon to denounce their erstwhile friend as stupid if not actually dishonest. Or turn to the realm of politics. How simple the difficulties of the minister in comparison with those of the office-holder! One November day in 1863 Abraham Lincoln stood on the battlefield at Gettysburg and read a brief address dedicating the area as a burial place for Union soldiers. That address is now recognized as one of the masterpieces of English prose. But how furiously it was condemned at the time! The next day a hostile newspaper in Harrisburg, Pennsylvania, published this incredible comment. "We pass over the silly remarks of the President. For the credit of America we hope the veil of oblivion will be dropped over them, and that never again will they be repeated or even thought of." Managing personal antagonisms—surely the problem is familiar to every man in public life!

Unhappily there are many people not in public life who face this same problem. In most families antagonisms eventually develop, antagonisms which sometimes lead to permanent and violent antipathies. Occasionally these domestic quarrels are concealed from outsiders: more often they become painfully familiar to neighbors and friends. Sometimes the resultant feuds are eventually forgotten: sometimes they persist—even to the second and third generations. It was, apparently, such a family-quarrel which gave one of our poets the idea for this highly original poem.

> Some say the world will end in fire,
> Some say in ice.
> From what I've tasted of desire
> I hold with those who favor fire.
> But if it had to perish twice
> I think I know enough of hate
> To know that for destruction, ice
> Is also great,
> And would suffice.[1]

What is the secret of managing personal antagonisms? How should we meet them, and what can we do to assuage the hostility of which they are a product and a symbol?

II

Whenever we encounter hatred, or even mild dislike, we should remind ourselves of this fact. There are many antagonisms which can be, should be, and must be quietly ignored. We make a sorry blunder if we permit them to wreck our peace of mind or interrupt the work we are trying to do. Consider, for example, the antagonisms which grow out of ignorance. The letter we quoted at the beginning of this chapter reveals an antagonism of this type. The writer of the letter knows so little about ministers that he lumps together for generalized denunciation a Protestant liberal, a Protestant fundamentalist, a Roman Catholic, and the unclassifiable leader of a California cult. The comments of a man who knows so little about the profession and the individuals he is thus berating can be, and should be, entirely ignored. Or consider the antagonisms which are rooted in envy. Here is a woman who is happily married and whose children are an obvious credit to her and to the community. Next door, on one side, lives a woman who has never been married at all; and next door, on the other side, lives a woman whose marriage has been a bitter disappointment. Presently there is hard feeling between these three neighbors. The woman whose children are attractive and well-bred is secretly denounced by the other two women, and their criticisms naturally wound her deeply. What is the ultimate source of this unhappy antagonism? Envy—the envy felt by an unmarried woman toward a woman who is married, and the envy felt by a mother who has failed toward a mother who has succeeded. Such antagonisms must not be taken too seriously. They must be analyzed, understood, and then ignored.

Similarly we must teach ourselves to overlook the antagonisms which emerge when one individual is forced to punish, discipline, or supplant another. To expect friendliness and good will in such situations is to show a surprising ignorance of human nature. Resentment is almost certain, and when it appears it must be quietly overlooked. Some two hundred and fifty years ago an English clergyman named Fell came into a position of authority at Oxford University. He immediately introduced a series of much-needed and long-awaited reforms. He compelled the students to attend their classes, he stiffened all the examinations, and he ruthlessly expelled boys who had shown themselves habitual trouble-makers. Naturally Dean Fell was not over-popular with the undergraduates, and one day an obstreperous youngster named Tom Brown rattled off a rhyme which the world has been laughing at ever since:

> I do not love thee, Dr. Fell,
> The reason why I cannot tell;
> But this alone I know full well,
> I do not love thee, Dr. Fell!

Did the Dean need to worry over this indictment? Certainly not! It came from a student who was on the verge of expulsion, and who was naturally hostile to the man who did the expelling.

III

After we have thus taught ourselves to ignore some of the antagonisms we encounter, we should go on and teach ourselves to study the remaining antagonisms in their true proportions and in an accurate perspective. Most people, finding they are criticized, promptly lose their emotional balance and with it their capacity for discriminating judgment. Learning that some people who read their last book disagreed violently with it, they tell themselves bitterly that no one liked the book. But how hasty and unfounded that conclusion! There may have been scores of readers—and readers who are not of the letter-writing variety—for whom the book was a light shining in a dark place. Or hearing that one of their friends has circulated a mean bit of gossip about them, they immediately denounce that friend as a contemptible traitor. But how unfair that verdict! After all, jesting remarks are sometimes misunderstood and misreported. After all, people sometimes say things one day which they bitterly regret the next. After all, stories which come to us at second, third, or tenth hand must be heavily discounted. If all of us would make it a rule to see antagonisms in their true proportions, study antipathies in an accurate perspective, we could by this single effort eliminate from our lives fully half of our quarrels and nearly half our unhappiness.

Two generations ago an indignant Bostonian rushed to Dr. Edward Everett's house and demanded an immediate interview. One of the local papers had published an article criticizing this man and his work, and now he was beside himself with rage and excitement. Should he demand a public apology from the editor, or file a suit for damages? Dr. Everett listened quietly for a few moments, and then interrupted the man's hysterical ramblings. "What should you do? My dear sir, do nothing! Half the people who read that paper never saw the article about you. Half of those who did see it failed to read it. Half of those who read it did not understand it. Half of those who understood it did not believe it. Half of those who believed it were people of no consequence anyway." There spoke a man who had learned to maintain his sense of proportion, his ability to study a conflict dispassionately. Would that all of us possessed his power!

IV

When we have completed these two disciplines we may well undertake a third. At any cost in effort we must banish from our mind all resentment toward the people who have mistreated us. We must purge ourselves of all bitterness, all malice, all desire for revenge. Why is such an effort essential? Because resentment, even resentment which is justified, works havoc in our own inner life. Show me a man who will not forgive and forget, who is forever scheming to repay the alleged friend who tricked him, who treasures secret grudges against his own children; and I will show you a man who will eventually become a desperate problem for himself as well as for everyone in his vicinity. You and I cannot think steadily and accurately if violent resentments are forever surging into our mind and upsetting its delicate mechanisms. We cannot maintain our inward quietness if bitter memories are forever touching off emotional explosions within us. At some unlucky moment, and on an incredibly inadequate provocation, we are likely to fly into a passion of vindictive rage. Even though we may then be lucky enough to control our fists, we shall probably not have enough self-mastery to control our tongue; and in the succeeding instants we shall probably say things which later we would give literally anything to have unsaid. "Forgive seventy times seven" [2]—Jesus' old rule is still profoundly significant. Only as we forgive habitually, only as we keep ourselves free from all inward bitterness, can we master life and make ourselves safe members of our community.

You say you could never lay aside *all* resentments? That there are a few antagonisms you could never

[2] Matthew 18:22.

abandon? Listen to the story of a colored man who has succeeded at the very point where you are failing. In 1909 a young teacher named Laurence Jones settled in a poverty-stricken community in the Black Belt of Mississippi. The town was called Braxton, and the children there were some of the neediest and most ignorant in the entire South. Jones had worked his way through Iowa State University, and now was eager to organize a school in this underprivileged area. No building was available, and he was obliged to hold the first sessions of his school in the open air —under a huge cedar tree. Eventually he secured the use of an abandoned cabin, drove out the bats and the owls that were nesting there, put a new roof on the building, and then moved his pupils indoors. For the next eight years Jones gave his very life to the task of teaching those needy youngsters and their parents. Under his efforts the level of the whole community began to rise. Then, wholly unexpectedly, a near-tragedy overtook him.

One night a crowd of white ruffians, many of them drunk, set out on a lynching party. Jones was the negro they happened to meet. Ironically enough, he was at the time walking home from a little church in which he had been preaching. He was seized by this disreputable gang, dragged to a huge tree, and there asked jeeringly if he had anything to say before he was lynched. He explained quietly that he was teacher, a graduate of a white man's college. Then he told the story of the Braxton school, and explained how much help it had already brought to hundreds of colored children. As he recounted the struggles of the preceding eight years, the men who had planned to lynch him began to creep away silently into the surrounding darkness. Finally Jones found himself entirely alone, the lynchers' noose still resting on his shoulders. He shook off the rope, and walked home to Braxton. He was later asked if he did not hate the men who had nearly murdered him. His reply is infinitely suggestive. "I'm too busy running my school to think about them. I haven't time to hate anybody." [2] Other people have learned to forgive and forget. You and I must do that too.

V

But this problem of managing personal antagonisms is only half solved when we have taught

[2] See *Collier's Weekly* for August 30, 1924.

ourselves to endure hostility without bitterness. We must go on and try to change our enemies into friends. It is not enough, when we are reviled, merely to refrain from reviling back. We must learn how to alter the attitude of the man who has been reviling us, win him from hostility to good will. What is the secret of this achievement?

Suppose we confess at the outset that there are, as we said earlier in this chapter, certain individuals whose friendliness we can never gain. Dean Fell at Oxford found it frankly impossible to win the approval of the students whom he had to discipline. The woman who had a happy home and attractive children found it equally difficult to turn her jealous neighbors into enthusiastic admirers. There were individuals in ancient Galilee whose good will Jesus could not gain. You and I must not expect to win universal popularity. It has never been gained by any human being, and in all probability it never will be. Yet when we have admitted frankly there are some enemies who can never be transformed into friends, some critics who can never be manipulated into admirers, the important point is still to be stated. Many hatreds can be obliterated.

Many antagonisms can be removed. The group that dislikes us can be made smaller, and the group that is well-disposed toward us can be made larger. Centuries of human experience have proved this is true, and have shown furthermore the steps we must take when we seek to win this victory.

The first step is fairly plain. We must make it a rule never to criticize our enemies in public. We may think what we will about them in private, but no word of public censure should ever pass our lips. Why? Because there are, in every community, some individuals who take a malicious joy in repeating to one person what another person has said about him. Sometimes this reporting is accurate: more often it is maliciously inaccurate. Gossips, tale-bearers, and trouble-makers take a perverse delight in twisting words out of their original meaning, expanding criticisms, minimizing friendly judgments; and then continuing the effort until old antipathies are reawakened and new antagonisms aroused. All of us must learn, if we seek to change enemies into friends, to preserve a discreet and an unbroken silence about the individuals who are hostile to us. Enmities can never be healed in an atmosphere of tension and suspicion, or in the midst of a storm of attack, counter-attack, and renewed offensive. When Robert E. Lee was a cadet at West Point one of his classmates took a violent and a wholly irrational dislike to him. The animosity persisted not only through student days, but on into later life. For many years this fellow-officer made persistent and malicious attacks on Lee's record and character. One day a mutual acquaintance, speaking with apparent friendliness, asked Lee what he thought of this hostile individual. To the questioner's surprise, Lee spoke in the highest terms of him. Then the questioner retorted slyly, "I guess you don't know what he's been saying about you for years." But Lee avoided the trap skilfully. "You have not asked me," he said, "for his opinion of me. You have asked me for my opinion of him." As far as Lee was concerned, the feud could not be perpetuated. Tale-bearers could find no material out of which to create further misunderstanding and bitterness.

We shall also do well, as we try to change enemies into friends, to remember that the people who are hostile to us may, at any moment and without the slightest warning, begin to change their opinion of us and alter their attitude toward us. We usually imagine that our enemies are strange and rigid creatures whose feelings never change. But how false this notion is! Our enemies are quite as changeable, quite as plastic, as we are. At any moment they may realize they have misjudged us and mistreated us, and may resolve to do the kindly rather than the hateful thing. How many situations there are which precipitate such changes of inner attitude—in our enemies as well as in ourselves! Sometimes old and bitter memories fade, and in fading slowly carry away ancient antagonisms. Sometimes new and unexpected responsibilities emerge, and in emerging compel erstwhile enemies to work together and gain a new mutual understanding. Sometimes the secret sources of emotion are opened, and a wave of feeling suddenly detaches the individual from the bitterness and resentment to which he has been affixed for years. In any or all of these ways changes may be wrought in the inner life of human beings, and swift and radical readjustments may be precipitated in their beliefs, attitudes, and habit-patterns.

Some years ago a delinquent girl who was a particularly difficult problem for the authorities was placed in a reformatory near New York. The matron there had been unusually successful in dealing with cases of this type, but Kate—the new girl—seemed utterly unresponsive to all her advances. One night a trivial but unfortunate occurrence threw Kate into a savage fit of temper. She screamed and cursed, and then began beating the door of her room. The matron tried in every conceivable way to quiet her, and then, when the uproar threatened to disturb the entire institution, reluctantly gave orders that Kate should be placed in handcuffs. The new restriction made Kate even more furious, and with her manacled fists she began to pound a wild tattoo on the door. The matron argued, pleaded, threatened, promised, and then—worn out by hours of unavailing struggle— suddenly burst into tears. Kate gazed at her in astonishment. "What yer cryin' fer?" "Because, Kate, I can't find any way to help you. No matter what I do I can't make you my friend." There was a long and a strained silence, and then Kate spoke in an entirely new voice. "That's the first time anybody ever shed a tear fer me. It breaks my heart. Take off these here handcuffs. Yer won't have no more trouble with me." Human attitudes do change, change in swift and unpredictable fashion. If we are in earnest about turning enemies into friends we must remember that fact, and plan our courses of action accordingly.

It is in the light of this truth that we see the profound wisdom of Jesus' rule for dissipating bitterness and conquering enmity. What was his rule? It was the rule of unfaltering kindness, unwearying forgiveness, unfailing good will. No matter how unfriendly other people are to us, we must always be friendly to them. No matter how cruelly they injure us, we must always stand ready to forgive them. No matter how persistent their malice, we must maintain in our own hearts the spirit of kindness. We must never seek to overcome evil with evil: we must always seek to overcome evil with good. Why? Because at any moment our enemies may begin to change their attitude toward us. They may be ready to change it even now. They may be waiting for only a gesture of good will.

> So we meet again after the years,
> The long, bitter years;
> Laughing this strained laughter,
> Speaking these trivial words
> About towns, books, friends,

So we meet again, and part . . .
O if you had held out your arms to me
I should have forgotten everything,
And come back to you, like a repentant child! [4]

[4] Adapted from a poem "Bond Street," by Lady Irene Butler.

CHAPTER VI

DOING ONE'S WORK UNDER DIFFICULTIES

I

ON June 3, 1887 a colored boy named Roland Hayes was born in an out-of-the-way rural community in northwestern Georgia.[1] Fate had given him the makings of a superb tenor voice, but Fate also piled in his path a bewildering succession of obstacles. His grandfather had been a slave and his father was a cripple, and the family was sunk in poverty. Furthermore, there were no adequate schools in the vicinity, and years passed before Roland Hayes gained even the beginnings of an education. When he was twelve his father died, and three years later his mother moved the family to Chattanooga, Tennessee. There she hoped Roland could find work, and there she planned to send the two younger boys—and perhaps Roland, eventually—to school. In a Chattanooga

[1] See Archer Wallace, *More Stories of Grit*, p. 40, Harper & Bros., 1930.

factory Roland located, at the age of fifteen, his first job. The pay was eighty cents per day.

During the next four years the boy discovered his vocal gifts and determined to gain, somehow and somewhere, a musical education. At the age of nineteen he started for Oberlin College, but the few dollars he had in his pocket took him only as far as Nashville, Tennessee. There he applied for admission to Fisk University, and there he learned to his chagrin that he would have to begin his studies at the level of the sixth grade. After four years of struggle at Fisk, he made his way to Louisville, Kentucky. There he found employment as a waiter in a private club, and began to pick up occasional engagements as an amateur colored singer. Eventually he met, at the club in Louisville, a man who promised to help him secure adequate vocal instruction on condition he would come to Boston and support himself there. In 1911 Roland Hayes finally reached New England —twenty-four years old, unknown, and penniless. Then began the hardest years of his desperately hard youth.

Hayes' first job in Boston was at the Brunswick Hotel, where for some months he worked as a bellboy. Then he located a somewhat better job at the main office of the John Hancock Life Insurance Company, where he was paid $7 per week. Just as he was beginning to accumulate a small reserve from this meager wage, he received word he would have to make a home for his mother. He found an unfurnished flat which rented for $4.50 per week, brought his mother from the South, and then from the rough box in which her few goods had been shipped built a bed for her and a bed for himself. After paying the rent he had $2.50 each week from which to provide food, clothing, and incidentals for two. It was amid such difficulties that Roland Hayes learned to sing.

The climax of his desperate struggle came in November, 1917. After long hesitation and against the advice of many of his friends, he decided to hire Symphony Hall in Boston and present himself in a song-recital. The recital proved to be an astonishing success, financially as well as musically, but of course the happy outcome of the venture was not known in advance. On the contrary, the days preceding the concert were the most nerve-wracking in Hayes' entire career. He was compelled to pay advance fees totaling $800, and in the effort to raise this relatively large amount of cash he set about the task of selling every possible ticket to his concert. He bought a second-hand typewriter, wrote two thousand announcements of the concert, and mailed them to music-lovers far and near. If enough people returned checks for tickets, plans for the concert could proceed. If the checks did not materialize, the concert would have to be canceled. It was amid such strain and anxiety that Roland Hayes prepared his program and struggled to bring his voice into perfect condition. Doing one's work under difficulties—how well he knew that problem!

Sooner or later, and in one form or another, most of us meet this problem. A day comes when we must do our work, perhaps our most important bit of work, under conditions that are cruelly unfavorable. Consider the experience of John Bunyan. In 1660 he was sentenced to twelve years in Bedford jail, and during the early weeks of his imprisonment determined to write a book entitled "Pilgrim's Progress." For that task he needed every possible encouragement and assistance, but how bitterly hostile his situation proved! Here is his own account of the anxieties which filled his mind as he tried to put his thoughts on his book. "The parting with my wife and children hath been to me as the pulling of the flesh from my bones; and that not only because I am somewhat too fond of these great mercies, but also because I have often brought to my mind the many hardships, miseries, and wants which my poor family is like to meet should I be taken from them. Especially my poor blind child, who lies nearer my heart than all I have besides: O the thought of the hardships my blind one might go under would break my heart to pieces!" Doing one's work under difficulties—John Bunyan certainly knew the problem. It was amid hopelessly unfavorable circumstances, in the midst of a cruelly discouraging environment, that he wrote the book which eventually made him immortal.

II

Suppose you are facing this problem today. Suppose you find yourself compelled to do your work, whatever it may be, under situations which are hostile instead of helpful. Suppose the very incentive and encouragement you most need are persistently denied you. How can you win your victory in spite of this handicap? What is the secret of maintaining one's power-to-achieve in the face of anxiety, weariness, and popular indifference?

Whenever we encounter this situation there are two immediate steps we should force ourselves to take. To begin with, we should make ourselves stop trying to explain our own difficulties. Our first impulse is to try to account for them, figure out why what has happened did happen. Sometimes such an effort is beneficial: more often it is distinctly harmful. It leads to introspection, self-pity, and vain regret; and almost invariably it creates within us a dangerous mood of confusion and despair. Many of life's hard situations *cannot* be explained. They can only be endured, mastered, and gradually forgotten. Once we learn this truth, once we resolve to use all our energies managing life rather than trying to explain life, we take the first and most obvious step toward significant accomplishment. Consider the situation disclosed in a letter which Robert Louis Stevenson wrote George Meredith in 1893. "For fourteen years I have not had a day of real health. I have wakened sick and gone to bed weary, yet I have done my work unflinchingly. I have written in bed and out of bed, written in hemorrhages, written in sickness, written torn by coughing, written when my head swam for weakness—and I have done it all for so long that it seems to me I have won my wager and recovered my glove. Yet the battle still goes on: ill or well is a trifle so long as it goes. I was made for a contest, and the Powers-That-Be have willed that my battlefield shall be the dingy, inglorious one of the bed and the medicine-bottle." Could Stevenson explain his tragic situation? Not possibly. All he could do was stop trying to explain it, and then devote his energies to the heroic task of mastering it. That was the road of victory for him. It is the road of victory for each of us.

We must also force ourselves, whenever we are compelled to work under a handicap, to stop wishing we could change places with someone else. Here again it is an instinctive impulse against which we contend. Finding ourselves forced to work under difficulties we soon begin to gaze enviously at those who work, or seem to work, under ideal conditions. How easy it would be to prepare our program of songs if we did not have to spend time typing announcements of the concert! What a simple matter to keep our voice in condition if we were not worrying day and night over the sale of tickets! Such thoughts, flashing into the mind, hide a grave danger. They threaten to divert our energies from the actual work in hand to the fatal process of comparing ourselves with others, and thus generating envy, self-pity, and despair. Life is forcing you to work under a handicap? You find yourself thinking jealously of individuals who seem to have no handicap? Break that habit of comparison at any cost! It is secretly stealing from you the very poise, the very strength, the very self-confidence you need for victory.

Whenever Richard Cory went down town
We people on the pavement looked at him:
He was a gentleman from sole to crown,
Clean favored, and imperially slim.

And he was always quietly arrayed,
And he was always human when he talked;
But still he fluttered pulses when he said
"Good morning!", and he glittered when he walked.

And he was rich, yes richer than a king,
And admirably schooled in every grace—
In fine, we thought that he was everything
To make us wish that we were in his place.

So on we worked, and waited for the light,
And went without the meat, and cursed the bread:
And Richard Cory, one calm summer night,
Went home and put a bullet through his head. [2]

What a mistake to waste energy envying Richard Cory! He too had his handicaps. He too was doing his work under difficulties.

III

But beyond these obvious and familiar self-disciplines there are three other efforts all of us must make when our situation proves hostile instead of helpful. If you study the individuals who succeed in winning a battle against heavy odds you will find that most of them employ, consciously or unconsciously, these techniques. To begin with, we must remind ourselves that significant reserves of strength, spiritual as well as physical, lie hidden within us.

Professor Cannon of the Harvard Medical School has recently published a chapter [3] which handicapped

[2] Edwin Arlington Robinson, in *The Children of the Night*. Charles Scribner's Sons.
[3] Walter B. Cannon, *The Wisdom of the Body*, Chapter XIV, W. W. Norton.

and apprehensive individuals would do well to study He writes, "When an engineer plans a building he does not provide merely for normal stresses. He multiplies his estimates of probable strain by three, six, or even twenty, to make the structure safe no matter what may happen. This surplus strength is known as 'the margin of safety.' How now is the human body built? Is it set up with a niggardly economy, or have there been included in it safety-factors on which we may count in times of emergency?" Then Professor Cannon adduces an amazing array of facts, substantiated by his years of research in physiology. "The margin of safety in the normal person's blood-sugar and blood-calcium is nearly 100%. In the circulatory apparatus and the respiratory apparatus there are also large safety-margins. The human heart? Usually it beats at a moderate pace and puts forth a moderate amount of blood. But it is prepared at any moment to contract twice as rapidly and put forth per beat twice the normal amount of blood, and do so against an arterial pressure which may increase as much as 40%. The heart is thus a marvellously capable and adaptable organ, richly endowed with reserves of power."

Then Dr. Cannon turns to two organs which are less familiar than the heart and the lungs. "The busiest and most versatile organ in the entire body," he writes, "is the liver. Its powers greatly exceed all normal requirements. As a matter of fact, three-fourths of an individual's liver may be destroyed without interfering seriously with his bodily processes. The safety-margin of the pancreas is even more impressive. The pancreas produces the insulin which is required for the proper utilization of sugar. Fully four-fifths of the pancreas may be removed without ill-effects to the individual affected. The entire amount of insulin needed by the body can be produced by only one-fifth of the insulin-producing organ." What is the final conclusion drawn by Dr. Cannon? All of us might profitably memorize his encouraging words. "In the human organism there are admirable devices for maintaining the body's stability, marvellous provisions for protecting it against attack, liberal margins of structural strength and functional capacity. When we are afflicted, when our bodily resources seem low, we should remind ourselves of the powers for protection and for healing which are already present within us, and which are ready to start working for us at an instant's notice."

These reserves of physical strength are paralleled, of course, by similar reserves of spiritual and mental power. John Bunyan, imprisoned in Bedford jail and distracted by the needs of his family, wonders whether he can possibly concentrate his mind on his book. But when he begins writing, the power he needs emerges within him; and paragraph by paragraph his great allegory takes shape. Roland Hayes, burdened by innumerable anxieties, wonders whether he can sell tickets, typewrite announcements, manage a dozen personal problems, and at the same time prepare the program of songs on which his musical future depends. But when he undertakes these perplexing tasks, the strength to manage all his duties quietly makes its appearance within him. On the night of the concert he finds he can sing as never before. You are working under a heavy handicap? You are fighting life's battle in a desperately uninspiring environment? Courage! Your body and your brain were not designed for a carefree existence. Your spirit was not planned for an easy world. You were made to meet and master strains far above normal. When those strains come upon you, you have no cause for fear. You can face life, and any situation life creates, undismayed. It was for just such crises that your safety-margins were designed.

> We see a sorrow rising in our way,
> We strive to flee from the approaching ill,
> We seek some small escape, we weep and pray,
> But when the blow falls, then our hearts are still.
> Not that the pain is of its sharpness shorn:
> We find it can be borne.[4]

IV

Another effort we must make, if life forces us to do our work under difficulties, is this. We must teach ourselves to keep the different areas of our life and thought carefully shut off from each other. Have you ever enumerated the different interests and responsibilities, and therefore the different anxieties and burdens, present in the life of the average person today? Take the case of a young man who is just beginning a business career.

His business occupies, naturally enough, the forefront of his attention. If he fails in that field, disaster will engulf his entire life. In addition to his busi-

[4] Anonymous.

ness, he has his wife and his children to think about. They inevitably claim, particularly if there are difficulties in his domestic situation, a large share of his thought. Beyond these two major concerns, he has half a dozen minor concerns. His parents and their problems, his brothers and sisters and their difficulties, friends near and far in whom he is deeply interested, the welfare agencies he is trying to help, the secondary career he is seeking to develop as a means of producing supplementary income in times of emergency—all these interests are present, sometimes distractingly present, in his little world. His inner life thus has many component areas, as a broad countryside discloses a dozen clearly differentiated fields. His mind and heart have many sub-divisions of interest and responsibility, as a ship has many distinct and inter-connected compartments. Suppose life compels this young man to work, not under ideal conditions, but amid heavy difficulties. What is the power he must acquire? The power to erect high fences between those different fields, the power to build tight-fitting doors between those adjacent compartments. When those fences and doors have been built, and when the young man understands the art of using them, he can retreat from a confused and distressing area of his life, leave there the problems that belong there, enter another area, and work with perfect quietness in the new spot. Suppose the young man has never learned to build these priceless doors and fences within his own inner life. What will happen? A chance confusion, invading one area of his world, will speedily spread to every other area and finally overwhelm his entire life. On our ability to shut one interest off from another, one responsibility off from another, one anxiety off from another, depends to a surprising extent our ability to achieve under difficulties.

Occasionally we meet an individual who has gained this power to partition his inner life and thus control his complex world. What an amazing capacity for achievement such a person reveals! Some years ago a surgeon in one of our eastern cities was invited to address an important medical gathering in New York. The very day the meeting was to be held the surgeon's own son was stricken with appendicitis, and the surgeon was compelled to perform an emergency operation. The operation was unsuccessful, and toward noon the boy died. But that afternoon the surgeon took the train for New York, and that evening read his paper as he had planned. Afterward one of his friends remarked that he seemed somewhat pale and tired, and then the surgeon confessed what the events of the day had been. Centuries earlier a Hebrew prophet had faced a similar experience, and had won a similar victory. Ezekiel writes quietly, "In the evening my wife died: but the next morning I did as I had been commanded." [5] Where do human beings find power for such achievement? They find it in the acquired ability to shut the different areas of life off from each other, and thus prevent the grief and anxiety which fill one area from overflowing into the others. Ezekiel had acquired this ability. The surgeon who lost his son had acquired it. You and I, practising patiently the control of our attention and the mastery of our emotions, can acquire it too.

v

There is one other self-discipline all of us must undertake if life forces us to do our work under a handicap. We must give ourselves frequent moments of isolation and silence. We must learn the

[5] Ezekiel 24:18.

art of resting—resting not only the body but the mind and the spirit as well. Did you never realize that this is one secret of the body's extraordinary power? Listen again to Dr. Cannon of Harvard. "The organs of the body are not active continuously. For long periods, even during the waking state, our muscles and their controlling nerves are entirely idle. The case of the heart is particularly interesting. Most people have the idea that the heart is working all the time. As a matter of fact there is a definite rest-period after each contraction. When beating at a moderate rate of seventy pulses per minute, the heart is actually working only nine hours out of the twenty-four. In the aggregate its rest-periods total a full fifteen hours per day." [6]

How should we rest? What should we do during our moments of isolation and silence? Curiously enough many people try to rest by substituting one exhausting type of activity for another, one intense strain for another. In the end they make themselves wholly rather than partially tired, and then mistake the sense of utter fatigue for the sense of inner quietness. Jesus had a far keener understanding of human nature. Study his rules for resting—"Go into thine

[6] See Professor Walter B. Cannon, *op cit.*, p. 289.

inner chamber, shut thy door, pray to thy Father who is in secret." [7] Notice the reference to the closed door —to the attempt to bar out everything else, everyone else, and finally achieve complete isolation, complete silence. Through such efforts Jesus gained that sense of inward quietness and spiritual adequacy which enabled him to meet the innumerable demands of his exhausting life. You are compelled to do your work under difficulties? You are forced to live in a hostile rather than a helpful environment? Then you need even more than other people do moments when you are entirely by yourself, moments when your tension can relax and your tumult subside. Without such moments, deliberately placed in each succeeding day, your life will grow increasingly wearing. With such moments you can find—first in yourself and then in the God beyond yourself—the quietness, the perspective, the endurance you need.

> Go a little aside from the noise of the world,
> Go near to yourself,
> Listen. . . .
> Music, pulse-beats of life, whispers of love:
> They were there all the time,
> Like a brook that is under the ground. [8]

---

[7] Matthew 6:6.
[8] See James Oppenheim, in *American Mystical Verse: An Anthology*, p. 230, D. Appleton-Century Company.

CHAPTER VII

LEARNING TO ADJUST

I

A RECENT volume on personality-problems contains this interesting incident.[1] "Mrs. Slater and her husband were entirely different in type. She was orderly, industrious, and hard-working: he was an irresponsible adventurer. He had swept into her commonplace world with a glamor which thrilled her, and without seeking anyone's advice she had agreed to marry him. But within a year after the wedding she realized she was tied to a dissipated wanderer who could not be depended upon to care for himself, still less for his family. During the next few years Mrs. Slater and the children were frequently obliged to seek refuge with her parents, while Mr. Slater was away on prolonged sprees. Then, suddenly and unexpectedly, Mr. Slater re-

[1] See Karl de Schweinitz, *The Art of Helping People Out of Trouble*, pp. 29-33, Houghton Mifflin.

formed. He sobered up, took and held a steady job, and for four years was a model husband and father. Mrs. Slater was overjoyed, and proudly told her parents that her judgment in marrying Mr. Slater had been vindicated. Then, quite as suddenly and quite as unexpectedly, Mr. Slater resumed his wanderings. During the succeeding months he sometimes wrote home, and sometimes did not. Finally he sent his wife a tragic message. He had consulted a physician in a distant city, and had learned he was the victim of a serious and a progressive mental disorder. It was this disorder which had been the root of his trouble for many years. The chances were he would gradually become unmanageable, and finally end his days in an institution." What was the problem Mrs. Slater found herself facing as she read that distressing letter? One of the hardest, yet one of the most familiar, in life—the problem of adjusting to a new and an intensely difficult situation.

The problem which thus assumed tragic proportions in Mrs. Slater's life emerges frequently, though usually in less extreme form, in the life of most of us. In fact a human career might well be described as a series of compulsory adjustments—some trivial,

some puzzling, some demanding our last resources of
insight, endurance, and self-control. If you look back
over your own career you will see how true this is.
You began your adjustments the moment you entered the world. Confronting you was a rigid and
complex order of Nature to which you, as a new-
born child, had to adjust or perish. Around you was
an already-existing human society whose language
you had to learn, and whose customs you had to respect, or suffer severe penalties. As you reached maturity and began to earn your own living you found
still further adjustments insistently forced upon you.
You found you would have to adapt yourself to new
personal situations, ever-changing business conditions, perplexing social demands. Marriage and parenthood brought still more adjustments—many of
them difficult and most of them compulsory. You
had to adjust to the individual you had married, and
then adjust to a succession of children whose needs
proved not only more numerous but also more expen-
sive than you had anticipated. Does middle-life
bring any diminution in the number of compulsory
adjustments? On the contrary middle-life brings a
marked increase in their number. On reaching the

forties and fifties most of us find we must adapt ourselves to a dozen unexpected limitations and a dozen
unanticipated disappointments. In some instances, as
in the case of Mrs. Slater, these adjustments in middle-life are distinctly tragic. In other instances they
have, at least as far as onlookers are concerned, a
somewhat comic quality. Consider, for example, the
verse written by a middle-aged mother who had just
met her prospective daughter-in-law, and who had
instantly realized what difficulties the future held
for her husband and herself.

> The people people own by birth
> Are often very queer,
> The people people choose as friends
> Quite shock your first idea,
> The people people work with best
> Your common sense appall,
> But the people people marry—they're
> The queerest ones of all! [2]

Since 1929 this problem of adjustment has become
even more familiar than usual. The situations that
have emerged in American life have forced all of
us to change our plans, reconstruct our objectives,

[2] Anonymous.

alter our accustomed way of living, and endure as best we can a wholly unfamiliar set of inner and outer strains. Few of the men and women about us today have what they want, and few want what they have. Nearly everyone is asked to make the best of an admittedly unsatisfactory situation. "Man is like a canoeist undertaking a hazardous journey across a wind-swept lake. Wave after wave bears down on his frail craft. Some of the waves are small, but others threaten immediate and complete disaster. The man in the canoe must master them all, even the big ones, or perish. He must study each successive roller as it sweeps toward him, and then meet it in exactly the right way—dipping his paddle at the right instant, giving it the right twist, and putting the right amount of strength into his stroke. If he fails in any regard he is doomed. His canoe, caught in the sweep of a swift breaker, will inevitably capsize." [3] Those words were written in the relatively quiet days of 1924. How much more stormy the lake has grown in recent years!

It is an open secret that many people never learn how to make these adjustments. Confronted by the

[3] See Karl de Schweinitz, *op. cit.,* p. 4.

necessity for swift and sudden adaptation they do exactly the wrong thing. Some individuals, for example, attempt to run away. This is the technique of the young man who, finding his job is becoming difficult, resigns and seeks work elsewhere. This is the technique of the young woman who, discovering that marriage involves unanticipated problems, seeks refuge in divorce. Meantime other people, compelled to make adjustments, conform outwardly to their new situation but inwardly rebel violently against it. Within their hearts an ever-increasing resentment accumulates, and then one day—usually on some slight provocation—they explode in sudden fury. Why must they economize while other people have money to spare? Why must they make a home for indigent relatives while other members of their family persistently dodge the burden? Meantime still other people, forced to adjust, try to solve their problem by insisting blandly that the problem does not exist. This, unhappily, was Mrs. Slater's method of managing—or attempting to manage—her difficulty. "On learning that her husband had mental trouble Mrs. Slater flatly refused to accept the doctor's diagnosis. When the doctor submitted further evidence of her husband's condition she replied angrily that the doctor did not know what he was talking about, and that she would entirely disregard his opinions." Was this a solution of the problem? Obviously not. Mrs. Slater was merely making a bad matter perceptibly worse.

How should we handle difficult situations like these? When we find ourselves face to face with difficulties which cannot be evaded, disappointments and limitations which cannot be outwitted, what should we do? What are the successive steps in the process of making an adequate personal adjustment?

II

The first step is familiar to most of us. We must accept, inwardly as well as outwardly, our unhappy situation. We must force themselves to stop fighting against our limitations, and surrender quietly to them. Only as we yield to the inexorable, only as we accept the situations which we find ourselves powerless to change, can we free ourselves from fatal inward tensions, and acquire that inward quietness amid which we can seek—and usually find—ways by which our limitations can be made at least partially endurable. This was, of course, the course of action which Mrs. Slater should have followed. She should have accepted the fact that her husband was mentally incompetent, and then rearranged her plans and her expenditures accordingly. The middle-aged mother who had just met her disappointing daughter-in-law should have followed the same procedure. She should have accepted her disappointment quietly, admitted to herself that her son's fiancée *was* queer, abandoned all thought of having a daughter-in-law of a different type, and then set out to win the confidence and affection of this new member of the family. To accept the limitations we are powerless to change, accept them inwardly as well as outwardly, accept them permanently as well as provisionally, accept them hopefully rather than despairingly—to do this is to take the first step on the long, hard road of an adequate personal adjustment.

Why is this initial step so difficult for many people? Because most of us were told in childhood that the way to conquer a difficulty is to fight it and demolish it. That theory is, of course, the one that should be taught to young people. Many of the difficulties we encounter in youth are not permanent; and the combination of a heroic courage, a resolute will, and a tireless persistence will often—probably usually—break them down. But in later years the essential elements in the situation change. We find in our little world prison-walls which no amount of battering will demolish. Within those walls we must spend our days—spend them happily, or resentfully. Under these new circumstances we must deliberately reverse our youthful technique. We must gain victory, not by assaulting the walls, but by accepting them. Only when this surrender is made can we assure ourselves of inward quietness, and locate the next step on the road to ultimate victory.

> There is a peace which cometh after sorrow,
> A peace of hope surrendered, not fulfilled;
> A peace that looketh not upon the morrow
> But backward, on the storm already stilled.
> It is the peace in sacrifice secluded,
> The peace that is from inward conflict free;
> 'Tis not the peace which over Eden brooded
> But that which triumphed in Gethsemane.[4]

III

After we have thus accepted the limitations we are unable to demolish, we must force ourselves to see

[4] Author unknown.

those limitations in their true proportions and in an accurate perspective. As we make this effort we usually discover that our restrictions, perplexing and disappointing though they are, affect only a few of the areas of our life. In the remaining areas we are still free. Part of our world is still unspoiled. One of the common mistakes of disappointed, resentful people is made at this point. They lose their sense of proportion and perspective, and tell themselves that because some of the satisfactions of life are denied them no happiness can ever be theirs. But how distorted this view, how false this conclusion! Suppose you have lost your money, and that for the rest of your days you must practise painstaking economy. In the other areas of your life you are quite as happily situated, quite as thoroughly in control of circumstance, as you were before financial disaster overtook you. You still have your abilities, your interests, your wide circle of friends. The relentless prison-wall at which you are staring so bitterly covers only part of your world. Suppose tragedy has wrecked your home. Some of the people you love are still here with you. Why not put your attention on those who are left rather than on those who are lost? And your personal limitations—old age, weariness, physical handicaps? Stop focussing your gaze on those barriers. Think instead of the wide areas of your life in which you can still find happiness and opportunity.

A generation ago a little girl was placed in an orphanage in a mid-western State. Her name was Mercy Goodfaith, but the name belied everything in her life. She was sickly, ill-tempered, ugly to look at, and—worst of all—a hunchback. Some months after her arrival in the institution a childless couple came there seeking a girl for adoption. The young wife explained she wanted a child no one else would take, and the matron promptly called Mercy Goodfaith into the room. When the young woman saw the child's twisted back, her scowling face, and her embittered eyes, she held out her arms eagerly and said, "Mercy, you're the little girl I've come for!" So began a new chapter in hers and Mercy's life.

Some forty years later one of the officials who was inspecting orphanages in that same State mailed this report to his superior. "I have just been visiting the Home in such-and-such a town. The house is exquisitely clean, and the twenty children there seem unusually happy. I had supper with them tonight, and afterward we all went into the living-room to sing. One of the older girls played the organ, but every other child gathered eagerly about the matron. Two little girls perched on the arms of her chair, she held the smallest child in her lap, and I noticed that one of the big boys sat on the floor at her feet and held the hem of her dress tenderly in his hand. The children simply adore that matron. She is a middle-aged hunchback named Mercy Goodfaith. Her features are very plain, but you forget all about them when you see the light in her eyes." [5] Cruel prison-walls shadowed part of Mercy's life, but how free and how glorious the rest!

IV

The incident we have just quoted suggests clearly the third step in the process of adjusting to a limitation. We must remind ourselves constantly that no matter how unmanageable our present is, the future is definitely and invariably under our control. We can make it what we will: happy, friendly, radiant with achievement—or exactly the reverse. How clearly this principle appears in the case of the young

[5] See *The Survey* for March 19, 1921, p. 893.

woman who adopted Mercy Goodfaith! Her life held a tragic and a permanent limitation—childlessness. But bitter though her present situation was, her future was distinctly manageable. By taking Mercy into her lonely world, by forgetting herself in the task of transforming Mercy from an abnormal child into a normal one, she could alter completely the dark and silent future that threatened her husband and herself. The day she held out her arms to Mercy and said, "You're the little girl I've come for!" she began laying the foundation for innumerable happy tomorrows. Or think of Mercy herself. Though she could never correct her twisted spine or alter her plain features, she could create for herself a future that would be radiant with the affection of scores of needy children. However uncontrollable her past, however disappointing her present, her future was what she herself chose to make it. Once we grasp this truth and appreciate its bearing on our own life, the problem of making adjustments loses most of its terrors. We realize that, though we seem to be the prisoners of Fate, we are in reality its masters.

Does this power to control the future extend from the realm of inward happiness to the realm of ex-

ternal accomplishment? Can a man who is thwarted
in his career gradually outwit his limitations and
achieve outward as well as inward victory on some
distant tomorrow? The long record of human life
gives an unmistakable answer. Some of the greatest
triumphs ever recorded have been the triumphs of
men who, on a dismal day of youth or even middle-
age, found themselves permanently crippled; but who
before life ended made themselves a blessing
to multitudes of people near and far. Consider
the heartening achievement of Arthur Pearson, one
of the best-loved Englishmen of our own time.[*]

He was born in southern England in 1866. From
birth his eyes were weak, and by the time he reached
manhood he realized they might wholly fail before he
finished life. At the age of twenty-four his race with
blindness became serious, and twenty years later
it reached its last sad stages. When he was forty-
seven he heard the best oculist in Europe tell him
that within a year the last flicker of light would fade
from his ever-darkening world. The doctor's prophecy proved true, and in the closing days of 1913

[*] See Archer Wallace, *Men Who Played the Game,* pp. 87-96,
Harper & Bros.

complete and permanent blindness settled on Arthur
Pearson. How could he possibly adjust to that tragic
limitation? What chance was there that he could
accomplish anything significant in middle-life and
old age?

The following summer the World War broke out,
and within a few weeks blind soldiers began to
appear in the military hospitals near London. One
day Pearson was called by telephone to come at top
speed to one of these hospitals. The doctors there
had told a young soldier that his sight was permanently destroyed, and on hearing the news the soldier
had gone into hysterics. They were unable to quiet
him, and now they summoned Pearson in the hope
that he—another man who had lost his sight—might
be able to say something that would assuage this
young man's terror and despair. The visit to the
hospital disclosed to Pearson a new and a glorious
life-work. He would organize a special hospital for
blind soldiers, and develop a program for their re-
habilitation! During the succeeding months and
years he carried out this plan, and when the War
finally ended he had no less than 1,700 blind vete-

rans under his care in a great institution at St. Dunstan's. He insisted that every man in the hospital learn Braille, that every man master a trade that would make him self-supporting, and that every man coöperate to make St. Dunstan's the most cheerful place in all England. Whenever any patient lost his courage and his self-control, and began to talk wildly of suicide, Pearson would visit the man, take his hand, and then say quietly, "You know I'm blind too." No one will ever know how many sightless veterans he rescued from death or insanity, or how profoundly he altered the future in literally thousands of hearts and homes. When he died in 1921 all England rose to do him honor. One eulogist termed him "The Man Who Conquered Giant Despair," and the Queen sent a great wreath bearing a card on which she had written with her own hand:

> Life's race well run,
> Life's work well done,
> Life's crown well won!

Your present is black with tragedy? But you, like

Pearson, can make the future radiant with achievement and happiness. Fate may be in control of our life today: we ourselves determine what our life shall be tomorrow.

CHAPTER VIII

DOES IT REALLY PAY TO DO RIGHT?

I

So far we have been discussing problems forced upon us by other people and by hostile circumstance. What about the problems forced upon us by the dangerous desires hidden within our own nature? Recently an eighteen-year-old boy gave an unusual account of this familiar situation.[1] Writing to the editor of one of our widely circulated magazines, he said, "Why shouldn't I, or any other ambitious boy, be dishonest? As far as I can see, being honest doesn't pay. Take the case of my father. He runs a store and he's always been straight, but where has his honesty got him? Ever since I can remember he's had his nose to the grindstone making a bare living for our family. A few years ago he ran for County Treasurer, and got snowed under by a slick liar.

[1] See *The American Magazine* for February, 1934, p. 44. "A Young Man Speaks His Mind."

He's grown old and gray before his time, and so has my mother. She's never had nice clothes, she's never travelled, she's never had good times. Now look at Mr. J., who used to own a store in the same block with Dad. During the War there was a shortage of sugar, and the Government asked the merchants not to hoard it. But Mr. J. bought all the sugar his big basement would hold, and then when the price went sky-high sold it at a tremendous profit. Later he ran for Senator and was elected. Then, as Senator, he got really rich, though we all know Senators aren't paid big salaries. Mr. Editor, I want to make money, and I want to make it while I'm still young enough to enjoy it. I think I can make money dishonestly a lot faster than I can make it honestly. Is there any real reason why I shouldn't be dishonest, or at least not too straight? Don't answer my question by saying that all the great men have been honest. I don't want to be great. I want to be comfortable."

Notice the exact question this boy raises. He does not ask whether it is wrong to be dishonest. He admits it is wrong. What he asks is why he should not be dishonest if dishonesty promises to be profitable.

What can we reply? How can we help him, and help ourselves, when an admittedly evil desire begins to push us in an admittedly wrong direction?

II

The answer to this boy's query lies in this significant fact. Before each one of us several different levels of existence lie open, each possessing its own set of happinesses and satisfactions. Between those levels we must choose, and when—consciously or unconsciously—we have chosen a certain level, we must take the happinesses and satisfactions that exist on that level. For each one of us life thus resolves itself into a choice, for better or for worse, between different planes of existence—each plane offering its own set of rewards.

We see this situation clearly when we decide upon a career. The boy who wrote the letter we have quoted says he will graduate from High School this June. What are the different careers that will presently open before him? He can, if he so desires, become a hermit and enjoy a thoroughly peaceful life in an isolated cabin. There he can sleep as long as he wants to and as often as he wants to, there no one will bother him by demanding that he help his community, and there he will be freed from the problem of earning money enough to give his wife a home and his children an education. Existence on the hermit-level has several obvious and definite satisfactions, and if this boy decides to be a hermit these satisfactions, and no others, will be his.

A second possibility opening before this boy is that he remain in his own community and live a thoroughly selfish life. He can, for example, take over his father's store, drive hard bargains with all his customers, refuse to share any of the wealth he accumulates, and finally amass at least the beginnings of a fortune. This career will, obviously, bring him distinct and genuine satisfactions. Misers do enjoy counting their dollars, men who have gained economic power do enjoy exercising it, and the individuals who accumulate a competence do enjoy giving themselves the comforts and luxuries our modern world so lavishly provides. On the miser-level this boy will find definite and demonstrable happinesses, and if they are the ones he craves the miser-life will be—as far as he is concerned—thoroughly satisfying.

But there is a third level on which this boy can place his life if he so determines. He can remain in his own community and live an unselfish life. He can, for example, take over his father's store and run it as a public-service enterprise rather than as a means for making private profit. He can show considerateness toward all his customers, he can share with others whatever surplus wealth comes into his hands, and year after year he can do his part to maintain the agencies working for the improvement of community life. Existence on this altruistic level will prove to have, as millions of unselfish people have discovered, certain definite and intense satisfactions. If, after careful thought, this boy decides that these are the satisfactions which he wants, he should put his life on the altruistic level and deliberately keep it there. Then, as the years pass, the particular type of happiness which he has chosen will be his.

> To every soul there openeth
> A high way and a low:
> The high soul climbs the high way,
> The low soul gropes the low,
> And in between, on the misty flats,
> The rest drift to and fro.

> To every soul there openeth
> A high way and a low:
> And every man decideth
> Which way his soul shall go.[2]

The same situation discloses itself, of course, in the realm of character. There again several different levels reveal themselves, each with its own characteristic satisfactions. Between them we invariably choose, and once the choice has been made we take, for better or for worse, the precise types of happiness which are appropriate to the character-level we have elected. This eighteen-year-old boy can, for example, decide to abandon all attempts at self-mastery and live on the level of habitual and uncontested self-indulgence. He can eat whenever he wants to and whatever he wants to, he can give free rein to his anger and his greed, and make it a rule to satisfy each of his other passions the moment it stirs within him. This is the animal level of existence, and if we study the life that goes on within the cages at a menagerie we can see the intense and thoroughly obvious satisfactions which emerge on this self-indulgent level. Slightly above is the level of incom-

[2] See John Oxenham, *Bees in Amber,* p. 19, copyrighted by The American Tract Society. By permission.

plete or occasional self-mastery. It is the level on which the average human being lives. The average person brings some of his impulses under control, and redirects to a certain extent the course of his instinctive desires. As a result he knows the mild joy of a partial self-mastery, and the faint satisfaction of an occasional victory over himself. Is there still a third level of character-attainment, with a third type of satisfaction, to which a man may aspire if he has the courage to do so?

Centuries ago Jesus said, "Blessed are they that hunger and thirst after righteousness." [8] Who are these people? They are the men and women who, whatever difficulties may arise, deliberately set out to win a complete and an unwavering victory over themselves, who finally place their life on the supreme level of thorough self-mastery and unwearying self-development. In this group we find the individuals who conquer not only gluttony and lust, but also the less obvious animalisms of fear, greed, and vindictiveness. In this group we see the men and women who seek social as well as personal righteousness, and who day after day lay down their

[8] Matthew 5:6.

own lives for the sake of the beloved community. In this group we discover those who dream of the highest type of achievement in their chosen career, and who deliberately set out to win ultimate laurels no matter how long and hard the struggle may become. Here is a level of character demonstrably different from either of the other two we have mentioned. Does it bring genuine satisfaction, enduring happiness? History gives a clear answer. The men and women who win a complete victory over themselves, who enrich life for others as well as for themselves, and who content themselves with nothing less than their own best, find in this daring and difficult way of life an intense and an abiding joy.

At the end of his long and arduous career Thomas A. Edison said with a smile, "I never did a day's work in my life. It was all play." After a lifetime spent in the battle against tuberculosis Dr. Edward L. Trudeau wrote, "The struggle has brought me experiences and left me recollections which I would not exchange for the wealth of the Indies." After a conflict which must have been as hard for him as it is for us, Jesus said to his friends, "Blessed are the pure in heart: they shall see God." [4] The high road does have satisfactions, satisfactions of its own peculiar type.

Now are these rival satisfactions equal in quality? Are the animals in the menagerie as deeply and permanently happy as the men who have taught themselves to achieve, and then made themselves a blessing to their fellows? Here is the very crux of our problem. If the eighteen-year-old boy who is hesitating between honesty and dishonesty will be quite as happy as a thief as he will as an honest man, then he may well spend time debating which career it will pay him to follow. But if the record of actual human experience indicates that the satisfactions accruing from a career of crookedness are usually far less permanent than those accruing from a career of integrity, then the wise course of action is clearly apparent. Fortunately there is an abundance of evidence on this crucial point. The most conclusive portions of it are offered, curiously enough, by individuals who have actually experimented with the lower levels of life, and who have found that the satisfactions avail-

---

[4] Matthew 5:8.

able there eventually prove distinctly disappointing.

Early in 1922 an employee in the postoffice in Pittsfield, Massachusetts, began stealing government funds. His methods were extremely ingenious and all traces of his theft were carefully concealed. His dishonest operations continued for several months, and he finally had possession of nearly $17,000 belonging to the postoffice. This was of course a far larger sum than he could have earned honestly during that period of time. How easy it was to be a thief, and a successful one! How foolish he had been to stay honest for years, working hard and receiving in return a niggardly wage! Early in September, 1922 the postal inspectors arrived in Pittsfield to make one of their periodic examinations, and after turning over his accounts this employee quietly slipped out of the building by a back door. So carefully had he made his plans for escape that the authorities never located even a trace of him. Policemen, postal inspectors, detectives, agents from the Department of Justice—all were completely and permanently baffled. The thief had vanished as completely as if the Earth had swallowed him.

But this was not the end of the story. Though the authorities finally abandoned the search, the fugitive himself began to be increasingly unhappy. The particular satisfactions which he had purchased at the cost of his reputation failed to make him happy. One day in February, 1927 a man with gray hair and a deeply furrowed face walked into the police station at Fort Smith, Arkansas, and said quietly, "I'm the man who stole the money from the Pittsfield postoffice in 1922. I'm here to give myself up. Hand me over to the Federal authorities." The officers stared at the stranger in surprise, and then consulted the photographs of the Pittsfield defaulter which the Government had sent throughout the country five years previously. "But you don't look like the pictures," they said. "No," the stranger answered bitterly, "I've had a lot to worry about. I'm doing now what I ought to have done in 1922. I give up." [5] Had the happiness available on the low road proved genuine? Not at all! It had turned to dust and ashes in the hands of the man who had given his all to get it.

All this suggests the answer to the question raised

[5] See *The Springfield Union* for February 15, 1927.

by the High School boy. He can be dishonest if he
wants to. If he is clever he may be successful in his
dishonesty. As a successful and well-to-do crook
he will undoubtedly find certain satisfactions and
happinesses. But experience has shown, over and
over again, that those satisfactions and happinesses
will not equal in quality the satisfactions and happinesses available on other, and higher, levels of life.
Such a statement does not rest on the prejudices of
parents or on the arbitrary say-so of ministers. It
rests on the century-long record of life itself. Here
is a hermit who has given his all to purchase a life
of perfect freedom and complete irresponsibility. He
has figured that the happiness available on that level
will be permanently satisfying. One day he sees a
man who has spent his life raising a fine family of
children, while the hermit has been enjoying self-
centered solitude in a mountain cabin. As the hermit
watches that father enjoying life with his stalwart
sons, the hermit's world suddenly collapses about
him. He realizes he has bought the wrong kind of
happiness, and paid for it everything he has. Here
is a thief who has won dishonest wealth from the
people who trusted him. The wealth is now his, de-

tection has been averted, and he—like the successful crook who escaped from the postal inspectors—
can enjoy life to the full. But one day this thief sees
a man who has been honest, who has won and kept
the respect of his neighbors, and who is admired
and trusted throughout his community. The thief
watches that honest man, notes the type of happiness
and satisfaction he possesses, compares it with his
own, and suddenly sees his dishonest world falling in
ruin about him. He realizes he has purchased the
wrong kind of happiness, and that he has paid for it
everything he has and ever will have.

> To every soul there openeth
> A high way and a low:
> The high soul climbs the high way,
> The low soul gropes the low,
> And in between, on the misty flats,
> The rest drift to and fro.
> To every soul there openeth
> A high way and a low:
> And every man decideth
> Which way his soul shall go.

There is happiness on each road, but the different
happinesses are not equal in value. One lasts forever: the others perish in an hour.

III

Suppose a young man recognizes the logic of this argument. Suppose he quietly resolves that he will, at any cost in self-discipline, master the evil impulses which push him toward the wrong road of life. What are the happinesses and satisfactions he can confidently expect on the other road—the right road? What are the rewards of self-control, honesty, and unselfishness in the modern world?

Suppose we admit frankly that the people who choose the high road today cannot be sure of amassing wealth. As a matter of fact many, perhaps most, of them will have to endure poverty. The wisest and best man in history was born poor, stayed poor, and died poor. He was, according to his own confession, in such need that one night he said to his friends, "Foxes have holes, birds of the air have nests: the Son of Man hath not where to lay his head." [*] We must not think, if we choose the high road rather than the low, that the high road will inevitably lead to a fine mansion, a large income, and all the physical comforts our over-luxurious world has become so

[*] Luke 9:58.

adept in producing. The high road may lead us, as it led Jesus, to the opposite situation. If wealth and comfort are our aim, as the boy we have quoted admits they are his aim, we shall do well to avoid the path of self-control, integrity and unselfishness. But if, on the other hand, we are willing to choose the high road and take whatever it brings, we can be sure of at least two satisfactions. They are so profound and so permanent that, as multitudes of people have discovered, they make the high road amply worth travelling, no matter what the hardship and the poverty through which it winds.

The first of these satisfactions is the joy of a clear conscience. To know there is nothing we must keep hidden, nothing we are ashamed to have known, nothing we would be embarrassed to see discovered —to know this is to possess an inner joy which wealth can never purchase, and which poverty can never destroy. Some years ago the editor of one of our magazines secured from a convict in a penitentiary an account of the convict's own feelings as he pursued his career of crime. The concluding sentences in the convict's statement are highly significant. "Just this to close. Even if a crook does escape the police, there's something inside him and outside him it's no use trying to beat. Death is mild compared to the thing a criminal always finds himself up against. I can't explain it." [7] What is this inescapable tormenter? It is the criminal's sense of his own guilt. Wherever he travels it goes with him. However successful his acts may be, it continually berates him. To escape from such an inward accuser, to face life and other people with a perfectly clear conscience—to do this is to gain an inner satisfaction that is beyond all price.

The other satisfaction we gain on the high road, and only on the high road, is the joy of meeting the expectations of those who trust us. How many such people there are, ranged about us in ever-widening circles! The members of our own family who have invested heavily in our future, the friends who would instantly defend us should attacks be made on our good name, the business associates who have risked their all on the assumption that we are worthy of their confidence, the still wider circle of neighbors and friends who look to us for honorable conduct and thorough workmanship—to meet the high ex-

[7] Originally published in *The Atlantic Monthly*.

pectations of all these people, to be the type of person they confidently expect us to be, is to know one of the deepest, most durable joys in human experience. In the letter we quoted at the beginning of this chapter the High School boy pictures his father as a man who "has grown old and gray before his time," and who "has always had his nose to the grindstone making a bare living for our family." But is this a complete and an accurate portrait? Surely, in spite of the father's hardships and poverty, he has known the joy of being true to his friends, the joy of fulfilling the expectations of his neighbors, the joy of satisfying the confidence of his wife and his children.

I would be true, for there are those who trust me,
I would be pure, for there are those who care . . .[8]

There *is* a profound happiness which accrues from such loyalty. If we lose it we lose, as millions of disloyal individuals have discovered, one of the ultimate joys in life. If we win it and keep it, we gain a satisfaction that is literally priceless.

[8] Howard Arnold Walter.

IV

How, once we have seen these alternatives, can we gain the strength of will to choose the high road and hold ourselves persistently upon it? What are the sources of the moral energy, the resolute idealism, all of us so deeply need?

We find part of the moral strength we seek when we analyze the right-versus-wrong alternative, and discover why it actually pays to do right. Once we understand the logic underlying high moral standards, the task of living steadily and heroically at our best becomes perceptibly easier. But our greatest source of strength lies elsewhere. It lies in the thought of the great company of friends and associates we mentioned a moment ago. As we recall them—their confidence, their trust, their high expectations—strength to choose the right inevitably emerges within us. You are facing temptation today? You need an added strength-of-will? Think of the people who trust you, depend on you, expect the best and nothing less than the best from you. The recollection of their confidence will turn your wavering resolution into iron.

On one of the reefs in New York harbor stands a lighthouse which for many years was tended by a widow—Mrs. Katie Walker. One day she told her story to a reporter from a New York newspaper, and he gave it to the world. She said, "I was living at Sandy Hook when I first met my husband, and he took me to the Sandy Hook Light as his bride. I was happy there, for the Light was on land and we could have a garden and raise flowers. Then one day the Government transferred us to the Light here on Robbins Reef, completely surrounded by water. The afternoon we came I said to my husband, 'I can't stay here. The sight of water whichever way I look makes me lonesome and blue.' For a time I refused to unpack my trunks and boxes, but somehow they finally got unpacked and I've been here ever since. It's almost forty years.

"One night my husband caught a heavy cold while tending the light. The cold turned into pneumonia, and they took him to the Infirmary on Staten Island while I stayed here to tend the light in his place. A few nights later, while I was sitting at the porthole there, I saw a boat coming. Something told me the news it was bringing, and I expected to hear the words that came up out of the dark. 'We're sorry, but your husband's worse.' 'You mean he's dead,' I answered; and they made no reply. We buried him in the cemetery on the hill over there. Every morning I stand at this porthole and look in the direction of his grave. Sometimes the hills are green, sometimes they are brown, sometimes they are white with snow. But they always have a message for me. Something I heard my husband say more often than anything else. Just three words—'Mind the light!' "

Hard for that woman to do her duty? Not when that message of trust came to her every morning from the hills.

CHAPTER IX

GAINING COURAGE TO ENDURE

I

In May, 1796 a boy named William Prescott was born in Salem, Massachusetts.[1] He proved to have a keen mind and an unusually retentive memory, and when he was only fifteen he was ready for Harvard. But early in his freshman year a tragic accident befell him. One night some of his classmates were enjoying an after-dinner frolic. In the course of the festivities one of them snatched a crust of bread from the table and hurled it violently across the room. Prescott happened to enter at that instant, and the flying missile struck him squarely in the face. He fell to the floor writhing with pain, and when his companions helped him to his feet one of his eyes was desperately injured and the other completely destroyed. For the next few months Pres-

[1] See Archer Wallace, *More Stories of Grit*, pp. 113-121, Harper & Bros.

cott lived in a dark room while the best oculists in Boston did what they could to save part of his sight. But the injury to the retina of the remaining eye did not heal, and finally Prescott realized that for him life would be a long and a losing fight against total blindness.

He completed as best he could his course at Harvard, and after graduation attempted to work in his father's law office. But presently his good eye began to give trouble, and after another stay in a dark room he risked a trip to the Azores. The oculists thought that the sea voyage and the change of climate might be of help, but after Prescott reached the Azores the condition of his good eye grew worse rather than better. For six weeks he was obliged to live in a room so dark that even the furniture was not visible. The only exercise he could take was to walk hour after hour around that black room, holding his arms outstretched before him to save himself from a collision with the bed, the table, or the chair. What a predicament for a boy who, only five years before, had entered college dreaming of greatness!

In 1820, after Prescott had returned to New England, he suddenly announced he intended to become a historian. Everyone who heard the news smiled skeptically. How could a man who was half blind dream of such a career? Prescott could never read reference books, or study source materials. Furthermore, the only essay he had ever written had been hastily rejected by the editor of the *North American Review*. How insane for Prescott to talk of being a historian! But in spite of the skepticism of his friends, and in spite of his own all-too-evident limitations, Prescott laid his plans and began his career. His first volume told the story of Spain during the reign of Ferdinand and Isabella. His second described the Spanish conquest of Mexico, and his third recounted the history of Peru. When, after thirty-nine years of literary effort, Prescott finally died in 1859, he had no less than sixteen thick volumes to his credit. They were so accurate and so luminously written that they brought him not only local but world-wide fame. How had he done his work?

The windows of his study had been covered with heavy blue curtains, and inside the room the dim light had been still further subdued by green shades. In that semi-darkneses Prescott sat six hours every day, while assistants read to him from a multitude of reference books. As they read he listened and memorized, and then scrawled tentative outlines of his chapters on sheets of paper he himself could scarcely see. Then paragraph by paragraph he dictated the successive sections of the book on which he was working at the time. During the last ten years of his life he was almost completely blind, and suffered excruciating pain within his fast-failing eye. But on he worked heroically, and when one day a friend attempted to sympathize with him he said cheerfully, "Don't think I'm despondent! I'm not. My spirits are always as high as my pulse—about fifteen points above normal."

What now was the type of courage which Prescott revealed? Obviously it was not that aggressive daring disclosed by a soldier, an explorer, or a financier who risks everything on a single spectacular venture. Prescott's courage was a quiet, steady fortitude—a bravery which enabled him to live year after year in his blue-curtained, green-shaded room, and maintain amid those depressing surroundings his confidence and his cheer. Centuries ago a New Testament writer said, "Some became mighty in war:

others suffered chains and imprisonment." [2] There are the two contrasting situations life creates, and there are the two contrasting types of courage appropriate to them. The first is the courage to conquer: the second the courage to endure.

> Courage is not just
> To bare one's bosom to a sabre-thrust
> In sudden daring:
> Courage is to grieve
> O'er many secret wounds, and make believe
> You are not caring.
>
> Courage does not lie
> In dying for a cause. To die
> Is only giving:
> Courage is to feel
> The daily daggers of persistent steel
> And keep on living. [3]

II

Suppose your life-situation demands the second type of courage rather than the first. Suppose the type of bravery you need is quiet fortitude rather than aggressive daring. How can you gain that fortitude? What is the technique of winning the power to endure?

[2] Hebrews 11:34, 36.
[3] Douglas Malloch. Copyright, 1916, by American Lumberman.

If you study people carefully you will discover that the power to endure is a product of two antecedent things—confidence that we can manage our present difficulties, and assurance that better days lie ahead. Let the man who is suffering chains and imprisonment gain the idea that he cannot endure his predicament any longer, or the idea that his fetters are permanent, and it will be psychologically impossible for him to generate fortitude. But let him come to feel that he is more than a match for his difficulties, and that some day his prison doors will open, and then the power to endure anything will emerge within him. Fortitude is the product of mingled self-confidence and hope, and when any of us need fortitude the thing we must do is start building within our own hearts a new faith in ourselves and a new confidence in our own future.

There are, now, three fairly obvious steps in the acquisition of this new faith and this new confidence. We take the first step when we remind ourselves that in every complex situation forces making for a change are not only present but continually active. We may not be conscious of them, we may overlook the evidences of their activity, and we may seriously underestimate their power. But there they are, and in the course of time they can be counted upon to modify profoundly the situation within which they operate.

If you look back over the critical moments in your own career you will see how true this is. Fifteen years ago you were face to face with your first major emergency. You thought the hard situation would be too much for you, but even while you were studying the situation you found certain elements in it changing. You discovered that new courage and new resourcefulness were emerging within you, and thanks to their unanticipated advent you eventually found yourself able to manage what had previously seemed unmanageable. Ten years ago another major crisis took shape in your life. Once again you were prepared to admit defeat, and once again secret forces making for a change altered your situation and suddenly gave you victory. That time a friend unexpectedly intervened in your behalf, and the disaster that had been threatening you for days suddenly vanished. Five years ago you met your third major emergency. What solved your problem that time? You have never been able to determine. All you know is that one of the many factors in the situation brought about a series of complicated and unanalyzable developments, and that finally you found yourself standing in bright sunshine rather than battling a terrific storm. What does all this mean for you today? It means you can face today's emergency without fear. After all, many different forces are operating within the situation that now confronts you. Any one of those forces might conceivably alter the situation. What if one of them will presently begin to do so?

> Once in Persia reigned a king
> Who upon his signet ring
> Graved a maxim true and wise
> Which, if held before his eyes,
> Gave him wisdom at a glance
> Fit for any change or chance.
> Helpful words, and these are they:
> "Even this shall pass away." [4]

Here is a fairly obvious cure for the discouragement and despair which have overtaken many young people since 1929. These young people complain that life today gives them neither scope nor opportu-

[4] Theodore Tilton, in *The World's Great Religious Poetry*, p. 598, The Macmillan Co.

nity, that for them the future holds only frustration and defeat, that theirs is in truth "the lost generation." They insist that because they were beginning their business or professional career just at the time the Great Depression swept over the world, they will now never have the chance to establish themselves securely in their early years; and that for them middle-life and old age will bring a series of heart-breaking but inevitable frustrations. What is the answer to this familiar pessimism? The present situation, admittedly disastrous, will not last forever. Many factors enter into it, and eventually some of them are sure to precipitate swift and far-reaching realignments. When those realignments finally take place the normal type of opportunity is certain to reappear. When it comes young people with disciplined abilities and well-trained powers will have the same chance they have always had—the chance to win a place for themselves in a world which has always sought, and must always seek, young people capable of leadership. Will it be too late then to make a start? Will the young people of today find themselves too old, when the new day finally dawns, to make a name and a place for themselves? Let us never forget that some of the noblest records ever made were made by men past middle-life, men whose early years had been a sorry succession of disappointments and defeats. Consider the case of Abraham Lincoln.

"Lincoln's boyhood was a story of handicaps and heartaches. As a young man he attempted a military career, and marched off to the Black Hawk War with the rank of Captain. But through no fault of his own he was demoted and returned from the War a private. Then he tried a business career, but a day came when his little country store 'winked out.' Then he tried surveying, but finally he was compelled to sell the compass and chain with which he earned his living. Then he entered politics, only to meet repeated defeat. He was beaten in his first campaign for the Illinois Legislature, beaten in his first attempt to be elected to Congress, and beaten when he sought appointment as a Commissioner in the General Land Office. He was beaten when he sought election as a Senator from Illinois in 1854, beaten again when he hoped to be nominated for the Vice-Presidency in 1856, and beaten still again in the Senatorial election in Illinois in 1858. But in

1860 Lincoln's chance finally came, after fifty-one years of disappointment and disaster." [5] No chance for the young people who reached maturity during the Great Depression? But there have been innumerable careers in which the darkest days came first!

III

We gain still more self-confidence and hope, and through them still more courage to endure, when we remind ourselves of a second fact. Whenever life forces us to go through a hard situation, life itself helps us. Wholly apart from anything we ourselves consciously do, secret forces around us and within us heal our wounds, restore our strength, reawaken our courage, and finally rouse us to reënter the battle. Some years ago one of the giant Sequoia trees in California was cut down, and scientists were given the opportunity to make a detailed examination of it. They counted the rings in the wood, determined the age and the history of the tree, and then published this interesting statement. "This Sequoia was a seedling in 271 B.C. 516 years later, in 245 A.D.,

[5] See John G. Nicolay, *A Short Life of Abraham Lincoln*, p. 552, D. Appleton-Century Company.

it was severely damaged by a forest fire. But Nature immediately set to work to repair the damage, and began to fold successive layers of living tissue over the gigantic scar left by the flames. This effort continued for more than a century, and by 350 A.D. the wounds had been completely healed. In later centuries two other fires damaged the tree badly. But when the tree was finally cut down, the scar left by the first of these fires had been completely obliterated, and the scar left by the second was in process of being covered. That last scar was a gigantic wound 18 feet wide and 30 feet high, but had Nature been given a chance even that wound would have been entirely healed." [6] You and I are not living in a world which injures us, and then does nothing to aid us. Ours is a world which brings pain and hardship, suffering and disaster, but then sets in motion ingenious agencies which quietly but steadily repair the damage. "The healing power of Nature"—how familiar and how beneficent it is! What help it brings, to men as well as to trees!

[6] Quoted in a sermon by Dr. Carl S. Patton, on "The Healing Power."

How does this healing power aid men? What are the things life does to help human beings through hard places? Life helps us by dulling our consciousness of pain, and by erasing from the mind the memory of acute suffering. Did you never realize you can recall joys far more vividly and in far greater detail than you can recall sorrows? Furthermore life helps us by disclosing within our own nature unsuspected capacities for self-repair. Who would have guessed, until after the first forest fire, that Sequoia trees had the power to fold successive layers of living tissue over the scars left by flames? Who would have guessed, until actual experience disclosed the fact, that men and women could regain their composure after a staggering bereavement, that they could recapture happiness after sorrow has devastated their little world? Most significant of all, life helps us by constantly piling new responsibilities, new problems, new duties upon our shoulders. Whether heart-broken people intended to forget their grief or not, they soon find themselves compelled to look out and not in, forward and not back, up and not down—and then lend a hand.

Home they brought her warrior dead,
She nor swooned nor uttered cry;
All her maidens watching said,
"She must weep or she will die."

Then they praised him soft and low,
Called him worthy to be loved,
Truest friend and noblest foe:
Yet she neither spoke nor moved.

Stole a maiden from her place,
Lightly to the warrior stepped,
Took the face-cloth from the face:
But she neither moved nor wept.

Rose a nurse of ninety years,
Set his child upon her knee:
Like summer tempest came her tears,
"Sweet, my child, I live for thee!" [7]

What a blessing that compulsory transfer of attention!

IV

But our greatest inspiration and incentive come when we recall a third fact. There is, hidden deep within each one of us, a secret self which is ultimately invincible. No matter how heavy our burdens, how perplexing our problems, how intense the

[7] Alfred (Lord) Tennyson.

strain circumstance throws upon us, that inner self never wholly gives way. Time and again we catch glimpses of it—calm, poised, unafraid. It looks out at us from some secret window of the soul, like a strange, brave face gazing from the casement of an unexplored castle. Do you know the origin of this invincible inner self? For millions of years it has been slowly taking shape. Our far-off ancestors were primitive men who faced a desperately hard life. They lived in caves, in forests, and in wild hiding places among the hills. Day after day they had to fight for their very lives—now contending against animals, now against hostile fellow-men, now against the furious and as yet untamed forces of Nature. In that grim and never-ending struggle the individuals who lacked either the will to struggle or the ability to conquer were speedily and inevitably annihilated. Only those men and women who possessed the priceless qualities of strength, resourcefulness, and unwavering courage survived. From this selected group the next generation sprang, inheriting these peculiar and immensely valuable spiritual characteristics. Thus through a blind process of selective survival human beings gained, bit by bit, the phenomenal capacities for resistance, for struggle, and for conquest which they reveal today. It was the life-process itself, working for millions of years, that created the invincible inner self buried deep in the heart of each one of us.

Do you realize how much endurance this inner self gives men and women today? Do you realize what achievements it puts within our reach, even though we are beset by sorrow and hardship? Listen to this fragment from the story of Mozart.[8] "In 1781 Mozart, a young man of only twenty-five, left his native town of Salzburg and settled in Vienna. There, ten years later, he died in abject poverty. Those ten years were years of almost incredible hardship, and yet years of almost incredible accomplishment. Mozart and his wife were so poor that they often had neither food nor fuel in their tiny dwelling, yet Mozart went on writing his matchless music. One day his publisher said to him harshly, 'Write, sir, in a more easy and popular style; or I will neither print your music nor pay you a penny for it.' To which Mozart, shivering with cold and hunger, answered wearily, 'Then, my good sir, I have only to

[8] Quoted by Daniel Gregory Mason.

resign and die of starvation. I cannot write as you demand.' But did those sufferings break Mozart's spirit? Did they rob him of his creative power? Certainly not! His three greatest symphonies were all written in 1788, during this very period of intense hardship. One cold morning that winter a friend who came to visit Mozart found his dwelling entirely without heat, and Mozart and his wife waltzing to keep warm." The invincible inner self—and it is in each one of us just as it was in him.

Once we recognize the presence and the power of this inner self we begin to understand what God's help is, and how and where it comes. Some time ago a woman in a distant community sent me this pitiful letter. "In one of your books you say that if we do our best God will give us the help we need. But what is that help? What if it doesn't come? For years my husband and I have tried to do right, but the harder we try the worse our situation seems to get. My husband would have a job today if he had been willing to be dishonest. But because he insisted on being square he is now out of work, our children are deprived of the things other children have, and we ourselves are worried almost to death. How can

I make a contact with God? How can I get the help you say he has for me?" What is the answer to such an inquiry?

The answer is this. The help God gives is not a sudden and miraculous change in the external situation. After we have prayed, and after the divine aid has come, the same problems must still be faced and the same burdens must still be carried. The help God gives lies inside our life, not outside. As we pray, God gives us a fresh glimpse of our own invincible inner self. The glimpse of that inner self, with its superb capacities for endurance and achievement, restores our self-confidence and quickens our courage. We suddenly realize that, even though the odds are heavy against us, we need not go down in pitiful surrender. Then, as we take up the struggle once more, God releases within us our own ultimate resources. A new strength, a new resourcefulness, a new wisdom born of desperation, a new determination never to surrender—all these powers emerge within us. The hard situation confronting us may remain, and usually does remain, quite as hard as it was before we made our prayer. But we ourselves are changed. We become inwardly invincible. In that change, wrought by God within the depths of our own being, lies the divine help.

> The outworks all are taken
> And the purlieus passed;
> But the keep remains unshaken,
> The gate is fast.
>
> I see them from the casement,
> The trampling foe;
> But this last wall's abasement
> They shall not know.
>
> Grief, hunger, madness, weeping,
> Prevail without;
> A central peace is keeping
> The last redoubt.[*]

[*] From a poem by Arthur Salmon in *O World Invisible: An Anthology*, p. 85, E. P. Dutton. By permission of the author.

CHAPTER X

DO WE EVER GET A SECOND CHANCE?

I

ONE of the current anthologies contains these interesting lines. The poem is entitled "Things That Do Not Return."

> Three things there are that come not back:
> The arrow shot along its track,
> It will not swerve, it will not stay,
> It flies to strike and wound and slay.
> The hasty word returneth not
> Though quickly spoke and soon forgot,
> In many hearts it lingers still
> To do its work for good or ill.
> And golden opportunity—
> That too will not return to thee.
> Thou mayest weep and plead and yearn,
> These three will nevermore return.[1]

All of us agree this is clever verse. But is it true? Do our opportunities slip away, never to return?

Some of them undoubtedly do. The characteristic

[1] See *Quotable Poems*, vol. II, p. 65, Willett, Clark & Co.

opportunities of youth, for example, are single-appearance affairs. If we let them elude us it is almost certain we shall never capture them again. We have only one chance to begin our education at the favorable moment, only one chance to make an early start in our career, only one chance to marry at such a time that we shall have the privilege of sharing youth with our own children. Here are opportunities which, as this poet reminds us, "come not back." But are they the only opportunities life puts before us? Even a superficial study of human experience discloses the heartening fact that there are many other chances which come not once but many times. It is the recognition of this situation, the realization that even if we have missed some opportunities there are others which are constantly reappearing, that has saved many middle-aged and elderly people from the despair into which older people readily fall. What now are the chances that come more than once? What are the recurrent opportunities of life?

II

Perhaps the most obvious is the chance to change our habits. Just now many people are saying that habits cannot be changed, that once we pass the golden age of twenty (or is it fifteen?) our habits become fixed and unalterable, and the contour of the self becomes as permanent as the sky-line. But such pessimists overlook one important fact. It is always possible for us to create new habit-patterns, super-impose them on old ones, gradually crush the old ones out of existence, and thus alter perceptibly the mechanism that controls our actions. How do we create a habit-pattern? By merely repeating one act over and over again, repeating it until a new habit-pattern is created. The number of our birthdays has nothing whatever to do with this process. Our intelligence, our patience, and our persistence are the only things that count. We can start repeating a certain act over and over again quite as well at fifty as we can at fifteen.

Here for example is a middle-aged minister who has always had difficulty making himself heard in a large auditorium. Finally he consults an expert in voice-production, and learns the exact causes of his failure. He has not placed his tones correctly, he has failed to use his breath properly, and he has not opened his mouth wide enough in the act of speaking. The voice-teacher suggests a series of exercises and urges the minister to practise them faithfully. The minister works for a day, a week, a month, a year—and finally his method of speaking is entirely altered. His earlier mannerisms are obliterated, and he finds himself attaining an entirely new level of achievement. Older people unable to change their habits? But every time we take any type of lesson we disprove this all-too-common superstition. For what are lessons—whether in golf, public speaking, French, or good manners? They are an effort to build a new habit-pattern, superimpose it on an old one, and eventually break free from the thralldom of the past.

When this fact is stated the pessimists retreat to what seems an impregnable position. They tell us that middle-aged people find it desperately *hard* to learn, and that even though it is theoretically possible for forty-year-olds to create new habit-patterns, it is practically impossible for them to do so. "You cannot teach an old dog new tricks"—and with the quotation of that time-worn formula the pessimists consider the case closed. But are old dogs as helpless as the proverb implies? Recently Professor

Thorndike of Teachers' College, New York, has published [2] the results of a significant series of studies relating to the learning-ability of older people. He divided a certain group of 465 adults into three sections, making the division solely on the basis of age. In the first group he placed the bona-fide youngsters who were still in the twenties, in the second the men and women who were in the thirties, and in the third the superannuated veterans who were in the forties. If each group were given the same tests which group would show the greatest learning-power?

To everyone's surprise the forty-year-olds came out first in every test Professor Thorndike devised. One of the most ingenious of his tests involved the ability to learn to write with the wrong hand. After many records had been taken, it was conclusively shown that the forty-year-olds made as much progress in this undertaking after only fifteen hours of practice as eight-year-old youngsters normally make after two years of practice. Professor Thorndike sums up the results of his investigation in these encouraging words. "We have discovered that mature people can learn practically anything they want to. In every

[2] See Edward L. Thorndike, *Adult Learning* (Macmillan).

mental function they are thoroughly plastic and teachable. In fact the learning-ability of older people is very nearly as great as the learning-ability of young people at the highly favorable ages of seventeen, eighteen, and nineteen." No chance to change our habits once we are past youth? But we have every chance! At any time we can start reconstructing our habit-patterns. They in turn will redirect the course of our thoughts, our feelings, and our actions.

> They do me wrong who say I come no more
> When once I knock, and fail to find you in:
> Each morn I stand again beside your door
> To bid you wake and rise, and fight and win.
>
> Weep not for precious chances passed away,
> Wail not for golden ages on the wane:
> Each night I burn the records of that day,
> At sunrise every soul is born again! [3]

III

Another recurrent opportunity, closely connected with the first, is the chance to discover and develop our own latent abilities. Here again many middle-aged people are the victims of a needless despair,

[3] Walter Malone, in *The Little Book of American Poets*, p. 240, Houghton Mifflin.

particularly in connection with their alleged "lack of charm." They tell their minister or their doctor that all the fine traits in a given personality disclose themselves within twenty or at the most twenty-five years, that they themselves are now far beyond that happy period of self-discovery, that they lack certain fundamental graces of mind and manner, and that there is nothing for them to do now but resign themselves to an admittedly unhappy old age of angularity and friendlessness. But how false this argument, how limited the observations on which it rests! The world is full of people who are far more attractive at seventy than they were at seventeen. They discovered within themselves, long after so-called youth was past, traits and abilities which increased enormously the appeal they made to others. They found within their nature a genial tolerance, a saving sense of humor, a quick sympathy, a priceless ability to listen while other people poured out their problems and their woes. Around these qualities they gradually reconstructed their personality and their methods of dealing with other people. As a result the friendships they craved and missed in the years under thirty gradually became theirs in the years after fifty.

Let me grow lovely, growing old,
So many fine things do:
Laces and ivory and gold,
And silks need not be new.
There is healing in old trees,
Old streets a glamor hold:
Why may not I, as well as these,
Grow lovely, growing old? [4]

What about the ability to achieve? Do middle-aged and elderly people ever discover that power within themselves? Here again the actual record of human life, as contrasted with the theoretical estimate of human possibilities, is immensely encouraging. Consider the story of John Davey, the man who won world-wide renown as a tree-surgeon.[5] Davey was born some eighty years ago in rural England, the son of a poverty-stricken farmer. When he was only eight years of age he was sent to work on a nearby farm in order to supplement the inadequate family income. After pulling weeds for twelve hours John Davey received the magnificent wage of sixpence. Schooling was out of the question: when the little

[4] From *Dreamers on Horseback* by Karle Wilson Baker, copyright, Southwest Press.
[5] See Archer Wallace, *Overcoming Handicaps*, pp. 94-102, Harper & Bros.

boy trudged home at night he was too tired to think of anything except supper and bed. The result was that at twenty John Davey was an illiterate farm-laborer. Had anyone prophesied he would later win an international reputation as a scientist, an author, and an educator, the prophecy would have been laughed to scorn.

One day in his twentieth year Davey was slating a roof. The slater who was at work beside him took a broken fragment of the stone and in tiny gray letters printed his name upon it. As Davey watched, the repressed ambitions of twenty years suddenly flamed within him. He resolved that, at any cost, he would make himself something better than an ignorant farm-hand. Two miles from the farm on which he was then employed he located a free evening school, and thither he trudged every night to take his place in a circle of little children who were learning their letters. Six years later Davey resolved to come to America, and eventually he raised and sold enough rose-bushes to pay for a ticket in the steerage of an immigrant liner. The following year he found employment as a laborer on an estate belonging to a wealthy family in Ohio. Twenty-seven years old, a half-educated gardener—what hope was there he could find within himself at that late date any significant ability?

Near the estate on which Davey was employed was a school which needed a new janitor. Davey applied for the position, and agreed to do the work free of charge provided he were given free admission to the courses offered at the school, and free use of its library. His working-schedule that winter seems incredible. He rose at three every morning and studied till six. Then he did part of the cleaning and sweeping at the school, then he did a full day's work on the estate where he was employed, then he finished the cleaning and the sweeping at the school, and then he returned home to study until his tired eyes closed in weariness. Why was he working so hard? Because he had·begun to suspect he had better-than-average skill in the handling of plants and trees, and because he was determined—no matter how much effort might be required—to develop that ability to the utmost. Years of study and practice followed, and then in swift succession came the days of Davey's belated triumph. The day when his gardens were admitted to be the best in Ohio, the day when he began to win nation-wide fame as a tree-doctor, the day when he published his book on tree-surgery, the day when he opened the school in which he shared his hard-won wisdom with younger men—these were his great days, and all of them came late in life. You say that human beings never discover and develop latent capacities for achievement once the golden hours of youth are past? But how many men are a living proof your theory is wrong!

IV

Still another opportunity that presents itself many times is the opportunity to make ourselves of help to other people, and in so doing win the happiness that invariably accrues from kindly action. Parents have the chance to give their best to their children, and then in the course of the years to give their best once more to their grandchildren. Does such reiterated kindness prove a burden to the men and women who give it? Certainly not! Some of the happiest people in the world are the elderly men and women who have had the chance to help successive groups of boys and girls, and who have made the most of this recurrent opportunity. Or think of the individuals who have transcended the narrow limits of their own home and their own family, made themselves helpful to an ever-widening circle of friends near and far, and in the process gained emancipation from their own burdens and disappointments. They have taken advantage of a recurrent opportunity life gives us all, and in doing so have found that fullness of life which Jesus discovered in his career of continuing kindness.

Eighteen years ago two middle-aged men were lying in adjoining beds in a sanitarium at Saranac Lake. Each was the victim of tuberculosis, and each had been told by his physician that an active career— even in the favorable environment of the Adirondacks—was no longer possible. One day one of the men suggested to the other that they clip from the newspapers and periodicals they were reading every fragment of prose and verse that spoke of courage and optimism, and then combine these quotations in a little publication that might bring cheer to other invalids. Gradually a detailed plan took shape in the minds of the two men, and with ever-increasing interest they prepared the material for the first issue of their new magazine. In one of Charles Dickens' novels they found mention of a quaint individual named Trotty Veck who earned his living by delivering messages, and who made it a point to spread cheerfulness as he went his rounds. His name was given to their new publication, and in April 1916 the first of the "Trotty Veck Messages" made its appearance. It was mailed to a group of friends, and the suggestion was made that anyone who wished to receive a second issue of the magazine send a contribution toward the expense of printing and mailing it. The response was so prompt and so generous that the two editors immediately began collecting material for their second number. Since that time more than twenty of these "Trotty Veck Messages" have been published, and the total circulation of this extraordinary periodical is now nearly 200,000 copies.[6] No one can compute the amount of courage and cheer the little magazine has brought to English-speaking readers the world over. No second chances in life? But consider the opportunity for helpfulness and resultant happiness that came to these men, and came to them when they were middle-aged in-

[6] See *The Knickerbocker Press* (Albany, N. Y.), December 23, 1925.

valids in an isolated corner of the Adirondacks! Here is one of the poems they included in the issue of their magazine which appeared in October 1931. What a meaning it has for the men and women who have come to feel that once youth is past, opportunities never return!

One broken dream is not the end of dreaming,
One shattered hope is not the end of all;
Beyond the storm and tempest stars are gleaming,
Still plan your castles though your castles fall.

Though many dreams come tumbling in disaster,
Though pain and heartache meet you down the years,
Still cling to faith, your secret fears still master,
And strive to learn a lesson from your tears! [7]

V

Are these recurrent opportunities limited to our present existence? Can we hope for second chances beyond death? We Christians are convinced we can. We willingly admit we know nothing of the details of a future life, but we believe that there will be a future life and that in it the growth in character

[7] "Harbor Lights of Home" by Edgar A. Guest. From Mr. Guest's book *Harbor Lights of Home*. Copyright, 1928. Used by permission of Reilly & Lee Co., Chicago.

which we see beginning here will reach its ultimate and logical conclusion. For what is the evidence the world discloses to any reflective observer? We find, to begin with, that the realm of Nature is in order, and that it possesses a significant ability to keep itself in order though its component parts are undergoing constant change. We find too that our world reveals a dominant element of beauty, and dominant elements of love and kindness. From this evidence we infer the presence in our world of a Living, Loving God who is responsible for the situations that thus confront us. As we study the long and complex record of life—beginning with the far-off day when our Earth took shape in Space, and ending with our own time when a perceptible advance in human character is taking place all about us—we infer the presence in history of a wise and consistent divine purpose. That purpose we interpret as the emergence of human life and the development within human beings of the higher faculties of the mind and the spirit. As we watch the individuals about us we note that each is caught up by, and participates in, this apparently universal growth-process. Every normal individual begins his career with powers that are obviously and pitifully limited: he reaches old age with powers that have been incredibly developed. All this—the presence of a Kindly God in our world, the emergence of a consistent divine purpose in history, and the appearance and development of significant mental and spiritual powers in every normal individual— is evidence of something. What is that something? What is the final figure in the design, the figure implied by the consistent pattern already visible before us? That final figure in the design is life after death, a continued existence and development awaiting every human personality. Our second chances end here? Not at all! We Christians are convinced that on the other side of death the same recurrent opportunities will emerge again—the chance to grow, the chance to help, the chance to love and be loved in return.

In October, 1800, a boy named John Todd was born in Rutland, Vermont.[*] Shortly afterward the family moved to the little village of Killingworth, Connecticut; and there, when John was only six years of age, both his parents died. The children in the home had to be parcelled out among relatives,

[*] See *The Life of John Todd,* pp. 35-37.

and a kind-hearted aunt who lived in North Killingworth agreed to take John and give him a home.
With her he lived until, some fifteen years later, he
went away to study for the ministry. When he was
in middle-life his aunt fell desperately ill and realized death could not be far off. In great distress she
wrote her nephew a pitiful letter. What would death
be like? Would it mean the end of everything, or
would there be—beyond death—a chance to continue
living, growing, loving? Here is the letter John Todd
sent in reply.

"It is now thirty-five years since I, a little boy of
six, was left quite alone in the world. You sent me
word you would give me a home and be a kind
mother to me. I have never forgotten the day when
I made the long journey of ten miles to your house
in North Killingworth. I can still recall my disappointment when, instead of coming for me yourself,
you sent your colored man Cæsar to fetch me. I well
remember my tears and my anxiety as, perched high
on your horse and clinging tight to Cæsar, I rode off
to my new home. Night fell before we finished the
journey, and as it grew dark I became lonely and
afraid. 'Do you think she'll go to bed before I get

there?' I asked Cæsar anxiously. 'O no!' he said reassuringly. 'She'll sure stay up for you. When we get out o' these here woods you'll see her candle shinin' in the window.' Presently we did ride out into the clearing, and there sure enough was your candle. I remember you were waiting at the door, that you put your arms close about me, and that you lifted me—a tired and bewildered little boy—down from the horse. You had a fire burning on the hearth, a hot supper waiting on the stove. After supper you took me to my new room, heard me say my prayers, and then sat beside me till I fell asleep.

"You probably realize why I am recalling all this to your memory. Some day soon God will send for you, to take you to a new home. Don't fear the summons, the strange journey, or the dark messenger of death. God can be trusted to do as much for you as you were kind enough to do for me so many years ago. At the end of the road you will find love and a welcome waiting, and you will be safe in God's care. I shall watch you and pray for you till you are out of sight, and then wait for the day when I shall make the same journey myself and find you waiting at the end of the road to greet me."

There is our Christian faith. Behind and beneath life it sees God's unfailing love. Beyond death it confidently expects the new opportunities which a Kind Father can be trusted to provide for all His children.